D0506853

Handbook of Small Business Valuation Formulas

Second Edition

Glenn M. Desmond
and
John A. Marcello

VALUATION PRESS, INC.

Marina del Rey, California 90292

© 1987, 1988 by Valuation Press, Inc. All rights reserved.
Published 1987. Second Edition 1988.
Printed in the United States of America

No part of this book may be reproduced or transmitted in any form or by any
means, electronic or mechanical, including photocopying, recording, or any information storage or retrieval system, without permission in writing from the
publisher.

ISBN: 0-930458-04-4

This publication is designed to provide accurate and authoritative information in regard to the subject matter covered. It is sold with the understanding that neither the authors nor the publishers are
engaged in providing legal or accounting advice. If such advice is required, the services of a com-
petent attorney or CPA should be obtained.

Preface

There are many reasons for valuing small businesses. Business valuation may be required in the following situations: sale, purchase, or merger; gift and estate tax planning; employee stock ownership plans; eminent domain; insurance planning; litigation and a myriad of others.

This book is written for the occasional user more than the professional business appraiser, although that group may also find it useful when valuing smaller retail and service businesses. Those who will find this book particularly useful are

- the real estate or business opportunity broker who is faced with a new listing and is attempting to set a price
- the small business owner who is considering whether to sell all or a portion of the business or who is attempting to estimate the approximate net worth at market value
- the prospective buyer who does not have detailed financial information for a business but wants to estimate the general range of value quickly to determine a reasonable offer or to decide whether an offer should be made at all
- the lawyer who is involved in drafting ownership or buy-sell agreements or who may need assistance in bringing bargaining parties together
- the professional appraiser who is seeking market information as a guide to forming a proper value conclusion.

This book should be used only as a guide to rule-of-thumb formulas, which may be considered along with other valuation methods.

Acknowledgments

The authors are grateful for the constructive assistance of the many people who have made a contribution to the *Handbook of Small Business Valuation Formulas*. The authors have benefited greatly from the personal experience of the business analysts of Desmond & Marcello. The contributions of Aaron Amster, Bonnie Baha, Vaughn Cox, Molly McCabe, Victor Richards, and Peter Zarifes have been invaluable.

Special thanks to Donna Desmond, who for many months researched, interviewed, and summarized information for this collection of small business valuation formulas.

We are also very appreciative of industry people who generously contributed their experience and expertise.

Robert N. Bolitho, Krehbiel-Bolitho, Inc.
Gordon Cannon, Farrell, Cannon & Associates
Paul Page, Service Corporation International
Jeff Silver, Industry Conference on Auto Collision Repair
John Hicklox, Hanna Carwash Systems
Dr. Vanderlyn R. Pine, Vanderlyn R. Pine Associates
Harry Franta, Home Center Magazine
Steve Ready, National Bicycle Dealers Association
Charles Link, Western Building Materials Association
Sharon Dye, Society of Collision Repair Specialists
Chuck Holahan, Publishers' Auxiliary
Jay Zircol, Zircol, Long, Ling & Trigueiro
Robert Hammond, Lloyd Howard Associates
Dawn Shapiro, Institute of Certified Travel Agents
John Vassiliades, J. Vassiliades & Company
Owen McCafferty, Douglas McCafferty Company Inc.
Dick Robins, Arthur Anderson
Bill Bishop, Bill Bishop Consulting Economists
Melvin H. Daskal, Daskal/Spector Accountancy Corp.
Jim Gibbons, Manufacturers' Agents National Association
Gary Lieberman, Granada Hills Schwinn
Ron Harris, VR Business Brokers
David Hales, Hales & Associates, Inc.
Sherry Sexton, Celebrity Properties
Richard Hubler, O.D.
Stephen Franklin, The Franklin Group
Daniel MacAlpine, Cutter Magazine
Sandy Hansell, Sandy Hansell & Associates

Contents

1

How to Use Market-derived Valuation Formulas

What are Market-Derived Valuation Formulas?

Rule-of-thumb valuation formulas have long been used, along with other techniques, to value small businesses. However, formula valuations are not substitutes for careful consideration and analysis of the multitudinous factors that affect the value of a business. Rather, they provide only one indication of value, when considered in conjunction with many other factors.

The valuation formulas set forth in this book are market-derived, taken from actual market transactions, or are traditionally considered "rules of thumb" used by a particular industry. Sources for the formulas include exhaustive industry research; data collected from accountants, business brokers, bankers, appraisers, governmental agencies, trade associations and others, as well as the author's own experience in valuing closely held businesses.

Different formulas are designed to value different assets or combinations of assets. Some formulas value the entire business (usually exclusive of real estate); some value just the goodwill; and some provide a combined value for trade fixtures, leasehold improvements, goodwill, licenses, and other intangible assets.

The use and composition of formulas may differ in different geographical areas, depending on economic conditions and regional business custom. The formulas described in this book provide a reasonably uniform guide, but investigation should be made to ascertain local differences.

Valuation formulas for small businesses fall into four basic categories

1

1. *Net Sales Multiplier.* The net sales or revenue multi-plier method uses the subject business's average monthly net sales over a recent period (such as the last one, two, or three years) and applies a multiplier appropriate for the type of business being appraised. The result of this multiplication indicates the value for certain assets of a going concern. These assets usually include trade fixtures and equipment, leasehold improvements, and intangibles such as the goodwill of the business. Inventory, cash, accounts receivable, and real estate (other than leasehold improvements) are normally not part of the value developed by the formulas.

2. *Monthly or Annual Net Operating Profit Multiplier.* This valuation method uses a multiple of average monthly or annual net operating profit. The assets valued are usually the same as those for the net sales multiplier.

3. *Unit Multiplier.* This formula uses a ratio of dollars to some appropriate unit, such as the ratio of gross revenue to the number of beds in a convalescent home.

4. *Summation Formulas.* This formula combines the results of the market multiples described in 1, 2, and 3 with the appraised value of tangible assets, such as trade fixtures.

Benefits of Using Formulas

Probably the most important benefit of formula valuation is the development of a test price for a small business. Market formulas provide a form of market comparison. Using the values indicated by a market formula in conjunction with other methods, one is provided with parameters of value within a range.

Formulas are relatively easy to use, and their structure makes intuitive sense to both laymen and professionals. However, values indicated by market formulas are valid only when other value criteria have been considered.

Cautions in Using Formulas

Formulas are general in nature. Many adjustments must be made to account for variations in sales and profit trends, location, lease, condition of the plant, fixtures and equipment, reputation with customers, suppliers, bankers, and others, special skills required, difficulty in starting the business, and so forth.

There is no single, perfect formula that will work for every business. Multipliers may tend to obscure details in exchange for ease of calculation to the unalert. The net revenue multipliers are particularly troublesome. They tend to neglect cash flow, profit history, and potential. It is easy to see how two businesses having the same annual net revenue may have very different cash flow. A proper valuation will go beyond formulas and include a financial analysis whenever possible.

The user of formulas is cautioned that all businesses do not conform to formula valuation techniques. However, some businesses may be valued by using a formula established for another industry where there are similar characteristics (presence of inventory, degree of labor or capital intensity, and cost of sales and profit ratios).

It is assumed that the use of the formulas will develop an indication of market value, that is, what a business could actually sell for. When valuing a particular business on a preliminary basis, utilizing information in this book, the reader should keep in mind that not all businesses are marketable. Thus, for many businesses, the formulas described may not apply at all. There are millions of small businesses in the United States, many of which are offered for sale each year, but relatively few sell as going concerns. A review of data from business opportunity brokers, accountants, business consultants, and our own studies indicate that only 15 to 25 percent of small businesses offered for sale actually sell. Most businesses simply are not saleable. The vast majority of businesses provide little more than a minimal salary for the owner. Others may be profitable but depend entirely on unique attributes of the owner, or have a short-term or no lease, or are restricted in some fashion. Many types of businesses are easily started up anew so there is no particular reason for buying an established one.

Important Factors That Influence Valuation

In valuing a business, a number of factors influence the choice of a multiplier and therefore the value of the business. Some of the more important factors are summarized here. Not all of these are of equal importance to all businesses, and this list is not intended to cover every situation.

Location

The location of a business is always important, but to some businesses it is absolutely vital. To retail and service businesses that depend largely on walk-in trade, and thus exposure to pedestrian and/or vehicular traffic, location may be the most important asset. Location includes accessibility as well as visibility.

Consideration should also be given to neighborhood trends. Demographic variables that should be noted include population density, household income, and age distribution. The valuator should analyze growth rates of these variables.

Lease Terms

Careful consideration should be given to the relative assurance that the business will be able to remain at the same location, by virtue of ownership of the real property or by a lease. If the business is operating on a month-to-month tenancy, it may not be saleable, even if sales and profit trends and other factors are favorable. In most instances, three years of assured tenancy would be minimal and there should be an option to extend the lease for an additional two to three years at a stated rent.

Competition

The valuator should examine the competition in the surrounding market and compare the services and products offered. Remember that some businesses perform better when there is competition nearby, particularly if the area becomes a destination point for certain kinds of products. Automobile dealerships often benefit by being in an "auto row." On the other hand, too much competition in the area will limit potential patronage and business value.

Longevity

As a general rule, the longer the business has been established, the greater the positive influence on value. The length of time at a given location is also a factor. Use caution, however, as some businesses become obsolete and actually decline in value with time.

Repeat Patronage

A business with well-established repeat patronage will tend to be more valuable than one that depends on more transient customers. Conversely, if the relationship between the customer and the business owner is a very close one, it may be difficult, if not impossible, to transfer patronage to a new owner.

Reputation

It is helpful to investigate the business's reputation with the public, established suppliers, bankers, and others. Does the business depend on the unique personal skills, abilities, personality, or reputation of the owner? Would current management carry on if the business were sold?

Covenant Not to Compete

Many businesses are not saleable unless the seller is willing to give a covenant not to compete. Such a covenant can raise legal issues that may differ from state to state and should be investigated. In the valuation of a small business, it is important to consider whether a non-competition covenant is an important issue. The valuator needs to determine what conditions are needed in such a covenant in order to support the value estimate.

Pricing Policy

The price of the product or service offered has a direct bearing on the level of patronage enjoyed by the business. If the business is basically a discount house, attracting patronage primarily because of price, then most other factors, even location, may be secondary. On the other hand, a discount business is often not saleable since it may be relatively easy for a prospective buyer to create a similar business from scratch by attracting customers rapidly through a discount pricing strategy.

Product Quality

The quality of the product or service is always an important ingredient in establishing repeat business. Does the business have a reputation for consistent product quality?

Appearance

What is the ambiance or atmosphere created by the business? Does the atmosphere generate patronage? Does the appearance fit the surrounding area? What is the condition of the store, the fixtures, the equipment? Is the merchandise clean, and well displayed?

Tangible Assets

Some tangible assets are included when a business is sold. Real property is usually not included, except in special instances. When using market formulas for valuation, all trade fixtures, equipment, tenant improvements, lease, and goodwill are normally included. Current assets such as inventory, accounts receivable, and cash are not included in formula valuations. They are valued separately and added to the formula valuation to produce total indicated value. The important considerations in valuing tangible assets are age, condition, and utility. If there is evidence of obsolescence or a great deal of renovation or modernization is required, the business value may have to be discounted to account for the cost of curing such deficiencies.

Special Permits

Some businesses require special operating licenses or permits. For example, a privately operated liquor store could not be in business without a liquor license. In many areas some businesses, such as auto wrecking or salvage yards, cannot operate without a conditional use permit. The valuator should consider the degree to which special permits are transferable to a new owner.

Sales Trends

Recent sales trends of the business are important. What is the most realistic outlook for the near future? It is important to note that even if a business shows increasing sales during the last year or two, it does not necessarily mean that the same trends will continue into the future. Most business sales tend to be cyclical in nature: increasing for short periods, leveling for a time, and then increasing again.

An important consideration when analyzing sales trends is the ability of the business to sustain estimated sales increases within the limits of its store area, equipment, parking and, of course, the availability of additional patronage.

During inflationary periods, as was encountered in the late 1970s, a business that shows increasing sales in terms of dollars may not be increasing in terms of its customer base. The increased sales may be due only to increasing prices. A business that shows a leveling trend in sales may actually be a declining business in terms of the real value of money or patronage.

Profit Trends

What has been said for sales trends is also true for profit trends. Although the most recent year's profits are the most indicative, it is always a good practice to review the past five years of financial information.

In reviewing financial documents, pay special attention to such areas as

- nonrecurring and nonoperational income and expenses
- owner compensation (salary, company car, company-paid insurance, and so forth)
- lease payments and remaining lease term
- interest expense
- depreciation and amortization
- pension plan contribution expense

Financial statements may reflect abnormal expenses for repair and maintenance, professional services, interest, insurance, and other items. Unusually high or low expenses should be normalized and a pro forma statement prepared. Additionally, nonoperating income or nonbusiness expenses may be present. These generally appear as income from interest or dividends, sale proceeds of an asset no longer needed or replaced, or expense accounts for automotive, travel, and other personal expenses. Reported income and expenses should be adjusted to excise the effects of nonoperating and nonbusiness income and expense items.

Development of reasonable owner's compensation expense is vital to the development of a pro forma income and expense statement. Proprietorships do not report compensation for the owner's labor on Schedule C of the tax return, but it is a cost that must be considered. Many profitable business organizations do extensive year-end tax planning in order to reduce taxable profit; this is often accomplished by increasing officers' compensation. Some owners' compensation may be shown in the form of pension contribution expense. This may require an adjustment.

It is important to analyze lease and interest payments in accordance with future expectations. Lease expense must be projected based on stated or anticipated future terms. Interest expense should be adjusted or eliminated based on the proposed terms of any sale.

Depreciation

Depreciation and amortization of tangible and intangible assets should be added back to profit before applying profit formulas.

Return on Investment and Return of Investment

Another criterion in evaluating a small business is its potential to provide a return on, and of, investment. Does the business generate enough profit not only to compensate the owner fairly for his or her services but also to provide an adequate return on the capital investment in the fixtures, equipment, leasehold improvements, deposits, and working capital required for the operation?

Criteria Used In Market-derived Formulas

For consistency, we have set forth market formulas using standard criteria. The necessity for such standardization becomes evident when we consider the potential for a wide variety of definitions and interpretations regarding the use of any formula. For example, the term net profit may have different meanings for different people. For small businesses, net profit may mean profit before owner's compensation, or it may mean profit after a deduction for a proper and economic owner's compensation, or it may mean net profit before owner's compensation but after deduction for business interest and depreciation expenses. The variety of meanings seems endless. The same confusion may occur with the terms gross or net sales, net income, net revenue, appraised value, and so forth.

To minimize this confusion, we have set forth the following guidelines to be used in conjunction with the market formulas described in this book.

Appraised Value of Tangible and Certain Identifiable Intangible Assets

We assume that the term *appraised value* means the value of the asset in place as a part of an ongoing enterprise. It is not the replacement value of the asset but rather its depreciated value as part of a going concern. It is usually thought to be the market value of the asset, used in conjunction with all the other assets of an ongoing business.

Some businesses have identifiable intangibles such as a liquor license, a franchise, or a permit. A value can often be placed on these assets based on available market information. For example, in some states, liquor licenses can be bought and sold in the open market, separate from a specific liquor store business. The prices actually paid for comparable licenses may be used as a basis for developing the appraised value of a license.

Cash, Accounts Receivable, and Inventory

Business valuation formulas usually do not include the value of cash, accounts receivable, and inventories in their results. It is assumed that the net value of these assets, if transferred at all, will be added to the result of the formula. Therefore, unless specified otherwise, you should always assume that the appraised value of these items is added to the result of the formula valuation.

Leasehold Interest

Leasehold interest is considered part of the valuation of real property and, therefore, is not considered in the formula valuation. A beneficial lease, with a contract rent below current economic rent, can create a leasehold interest in the real property and, of course, increase the apparent net profit or cash flow of the appraised business. Leasehold interest should be taken into account when appraising an operating enterprise, although it should be shown separately and not as an integral part of the business itself. In order to separate a potential leasehold interest from the valuation of the business itself, the valuator may substitute current economic rental expense for the contract rental expense when constructing the pro forma income statement. In the formula illustrations shown herein, it is assumed that this substitution has been made and, therefore, that no leasehold interest is included in these value illustrations.

Liabilities

No provision is made for liabilities in the formulas. If liabilities are to be assumed by the purchaser, then they must be subtracted from the formula valuation.

Market Value

We assume that the purpose of each business valuation is to arrive at an indication of the business's market value. Market value is defined as the most probable price in terms of money which a property should bring in a competitive and open market under all conditions requisite to a fair sale, the buyer and seller, each acting prudently, knowledgeably and assuming the price is not affected by undue stimulus.

Net Operating Profit

The net operating profit used herein is considered to be profit *after* an expense deduction for fair compensation for the owner's labor and nonrecurring and nonoperational expenses. The owner's compensation should be based on what the owner could make elsewhere, employed within the same industry, doing essentially the same functions, requiring the same special skills and experiences but having no ownership. Net operating income is also before deductions for business interest, depreciation, amortization, and income tax expense.

Annual Net Sales

Annual net sales are the sales for a one-year period after discounts, rebates, and sales tax. Net sales for smaller businesses are usually on a cash basis, and it is so assumed herein. Net sales are considered to be the same as net revenue.

Net sales are calculated before dividend, interest, and other income derived from sources not directly related to the business's operations. For example, a business may generate excess cash reserves that are placed in savings accounts or other investments that pay dividends and/or interest, and this may be shown as part of the business income. Income so generated is not to be included when using valuation formulas.

Correlation of Market-derived Formulas

In many instances in this book, you will find that different multiple formulas were used for the same type of business, some based on asset value, some on revenues, and some on net operating profit. These market-derived formulas must be compared to other approaches or methods of valuation such as income capitalization.

Developing a final conclusion of value requires careful consideration of the various approaches used. Weighing the quality of data used in each approach is extremely important in correlation. Those approaches that have a quantity of good financial data available should generally be given considerable credence. It is important to evaluate the data gathered from the market before selecting various factors or multipliers.

In instances where tangible assets such as property, plant, equipment, and leasehold improvements are the primary basis for value, proper consideration should be given to obsolete equipment, expensed items, or fully depreciated assets. Where inventory is a major part of the value, adjustments for obsolete and slow-moving items should be made.

Goodwill and Going-concern Value in Market-derived Formulas

Many of the market-derived formulas presented here indicate values for the intangible assets of an ongoing enterprise, as well as tangible assets (for example, working capital and fixed assets). Within this context, intangibles are grouped into one category. However, it is important to understand the two unspecified intangible assets normally included in that category: goodwill and going-concern.

Historically, the courts have generally agreed that an intangible value sometimes attaches to the tangible assets of an assembled business. This has been called *going-concern* value. Also, the courts have helped to distinguish this going-concern enhancement from its closely related brother, *goodwill*.

For most purposes, *goodwill* can be defined as those elements of a business that cause customers to return to that business and that usually enable a firm to generate profit in excess of that required for a reasonable return on all the other assets of the business, including a return on all other intangible assets that can be identified and separately valued (for example, licenses, franchises, and patents).

Some of the more common elements identified as components of going-concern and goodwill value are

—assemblage of property, plant, and equipment into a productive unit or units
— availability of trained employees
—systems, controls, and methods which have been developed as part of the operation
— existence of customers
— start-up losses that have been absorbed
— advertising and promotion accomplishments
— advantages of location beyond those directly attributable to the real estate itself
— local, regional, or national reputation a business may have established by virtue of public and customer knowledge of its dependability, quality of service and product, price of service and product, and credit standing with vendors and banks

In addition, personal goodwill elements that show up in the historical profits, but that are not easily transferred with the sale of a business are

—personal reputation of employees or owners with the general public, customers, other employees, other owners, and lenders
— personal skills of such individuals, including their technical know-how, sales ability, financial acumen, and so forth
—general skills of employees or owners in fields such as employee relations, customer relations, leadership, management, and administration

Definitions of goodwill may be influenced by special circumstances such as individual state statutory requirements and the diverse views of the courts, accountants, economists, appraisers, and others. For example, the generally accepted accounting definition of goodwill is the value of a business in excess of tangible and certain identifiable intangible assets. However, courts and valuation practitioners generally adhere to the definition of goodwill that was used in the case of *Houston Chronicle Publishing* v. *Commissioner* 481 F.2d 1240 (CA-5, 1973): "[T]he expectancy that old customers will resort to the old places and the expectancy of continued patronage." Basically, the generating of "continued patronage" includes both the bundle of elements called going-concern and goodwill. The term *going-concern value* was defined by the Supreme Court in a 1933 case involving the basis for rate making for a public utility, *Los Angeles Gas & Electric Corp.*, 289 U.S. 287 (1933). This case was referred to in a more recent decision, *Northern Natural Gas* 470 F. 2d 1107 (CA-8, 1973): "[T]his court has declared it to be self-evident that there is an element of value in an assembled and established plant, doing business and earning money over one not thus advanced, and that this element of value is a property right which should be considered in determining the value of the property upon which the owner has a right to make a fair return." Thus, going concern is an intangible that attaches to the tangible assets of some businesses. It may exist as a value enhancement for the assemblage of a business regardless of the business profitability.

The foggy difference between goodwill and going-concern value becomes more clear when we look at the measuring stick of each value. Going-concern value is primarily related to the physical assets of the assembled business and is measured by noncapital costs directly related to the assembling of the business assets. It may exist even if there is no history of excess profits. Goodwill on the other hand, is not directly related to physical assets but is generally related to the excess profits produced by the going concern. It cannot exist if there is no excess profit potential in the immediate future. Another way to distinguish going-concern from goodwill is that going-concern value comprises those elements of a business that, when assembled together, cause a new customer to patronize the business for the first time. Goodwill value, on the other hand, causes that customer to return.

2

Accounting and Bookkeeping Practices

Business Description   (SIC No. 8930)

Accounting and bookkeeping practices are smaller establishments that furnish accounting, auditing, bookkeeping, and tax services. They include the following:

— Accounting services
— Auditing services
— Billing and bookkeeping services
— Payroll and accounting services
— Public accounting and certified accounting practices

Valuation Formula

Valuation formulas for accounting practices generally are based on a multiple of the most current 12 months of net revenue. The multiplier ranges from 50 percent to 200 percent with 75 percent to 150 percent being typical. A revenue multiplier at the high end of the range would tend to be applied to a firm with a high fee structure, a history of profitability, a high client retention level, a good reputation, and longevity in its present location. The value indicated by the use of the multiplier is specifically for intangible assets such as goodwill. The value of unbilled work in progress, accounts receivable, cash, and fixed assets, such as trade fixtures and leasehold improvements, must be added to the value indicated by the use of the multiplier. Note that this formula may not apply to larger, regional, or national accounting and auditing firms.

Net Equity Value

To estimate equity value, the value of net current assets, restated at market values less liabilities, is added to the value indicated by the use of the multiplier.

Valuation Considerations

Among the factors that must be considered in the valuation of accounting and bookkeeping practices are: ease of transferability of the client base, the historical retention rate of the client base, client characteristics, lease terms, and revenue composition (that is, yearly audit fees, individual tax return clients, and other client services).

Transferability

Generally, in the sale of accounting firms, the previous owner/key employee will stay with the new firm for a period of time. Failure of the seller to assist in the transition will in all likelihood decrease future revenues. Key persons generally account for a high percentage of the total fees generated since they are most senior in the firm and command higher client billing rates.

Retention of Client Base

If the seller cannot assist the new firm in the transition, it is important to review the percent of revenues attributed to other staff members who can assist in the transition period to increase client retention. Studies have shown that client retention is greatest when

— the buyer and the clients are located in the same city, especially when the city is small
— the seller has served the clients for more than three years
— the seller guarantees a letter of introduction for the buyer
— the seller's gross fees have been increasing
— the buyer and seller are fairly close in age

A multiplier of 125 percent or higher of the latest twelve months of net revenues may be appropriate if all these conditions are met.

A further valuation consideration is the possibility of the buyer paying to the seller a percentage of the fees collected from clients who continue with the practice for a specified period of time. To facilitate client transferability, the buyer agrees to pay a percentage of all fees charged to existing clients for up to five years. In this instance, the true value of the transaction is not known until the end of the five-year period. The seller, however, should analyze the potential attrition rate for clients and apply a suitable discount to the anticipated income stream.

Client Characteristics

The types of clients served and their longevity with the firm are significant factors in developing a net revenue multiplier. A multiplier in the high end of the range is generally applied to a full-service company with an extensive list of long-term clients. The client list and workpapers should be examined to determine the quality of work, the reasonableness of the engagement fee, and the potential for increasing fees or providing new services. Of course, the ethical and legal aspects of giving outsiders access to various workpapers should be investigated.

The following factors should be assessed in evaluating the quality of the existing client base: industry diversification; geographic distribution; length of service by the accounting practice; maturity of the company; record of payment for service fees; growth potential; relationship with the staff and principals of the firm and type of services rendered. Practices with a significant percentage of revenues derived from annual audit clients rather than yearly income tax preparation should receive a higher multiplier.

Lease Terms

In valuing any small business, consideration should be given to the existing lease terms. The following items should be considered in regard to lease arrangements: amount of monthly rent, right to sublease, and lessee responsibility for utilities and other expenses. A long-term lease with an option to renew may add substantially to the value of an accounting business.

Revenue Composition

The actual number of clients and the fee dispersion may be an indicator of potential ease of transferability. A practice with only a few clients dominating its revenue base has a greater risk of decreased future gross fees due to attrition. One suggested method of developing a gross multiplier is to apply different multipliers to each segment of revenue based on probable retention levels. A sample of this application follows.

Developing an Annual Revenue Multiplier
Based on Percentage of Client Revenues

	Corporate		Individual		
	Audit	Tax	Tax	Other	Total
Percent of annual revenue	50	30	18	2	100
Typical multiplier	150	100	50	50	
Weighted percent	75	30	9	1	115

Example 19

Example

Step 1: Review and make a comparative analysis of income and expense for the previous three years.

Income and Expense Summary
for 12 months ending June 30

	19x6	19x7	19x8
Net Revenue	$362,811	$352,841	$387,482
Operating Expenses	282,360	274,560	302,235
Net Operating Profit*	$ 80,451	$ 78,281	$ 85,247

* Depreciation, excessive owner compensation, and interest added back.

Note: It is important to consider income and expense trends as well as the current year's (19x8) data. To more accurately predict future economic trends, the valuator should review the most recent five years of financial data.

Step 2: Adjust the balance sheet to reflect the market value of tangible assets.

Balance Sheet Summary
as of June 30

	19x6	19x7	19x8	Restated at Market Value on Value Date
Assets				
Current Assets:				
Cash	$ 20,114	$ 23,184	$ 25,186	$ 25,186
Accounts Receivable	119,249	135,790	143,180	130,500
Unbilled Work in Progress	7,443	8,490	8,375	7,760
Total Current Assets	46,806	167,464	176,741	163,446
Fixed Assets:				
Trade Fixtures, Leasehold Improvements, and Equipment (net)	68,554	65,188	70,142	105,000
Total Assets	215,360	232,652	246,883	268,446
Liabilities	98,423	106,840	111,583	111,583
Net Tangible Equity	$116,937	$125,812	$135,300	$156,863

Step 3: Apply the formula.

Formula Valuation Using Annual Revenue Multiplier

Net Revenue (Fiscal year end 6/30/x8)	$387,482
Annual Multiplier	× 1.15
Indicated Value of Intangibles	445,604
Plus Adjusted Market Value of Tangible Assets	
Current	163,446
Fixed	105,000
Total Gross Value	714,050
Less Liabilities	111,583
Net Equity Value	$602,467

Sources of Further Information

Associations

American Accounting
Association
5715 Bessie Drive
Sarasota, FL 34233
(813) 921–7747

American Institute of Certified
Public Accountants (AICPA)
1211 Avenue of the Americas
New York, NY 10036
(212) 575–6200

National Association
of Accountants
919 Third Avenue
New York, NY 10022
(212) 387–7066

National Society of
Public Accountants
1010 North Fairfax Street
Alexandria, VA 22314
 (703) 549–6400

Publications

Articles

Feeney, Charles F., "Buying or Selling an Accountant's Practice —
The Readers Response," *National Public Accountant,* July 1983,
pp. 20–23.

Gold, Michael H.,"Considerations in Purchase and Sale of an Accounting Practice," *Michigan CPA*, September/October 1972, pp.
4–5,7–9.

Neilson, Gordon L., "The Purchase of an Accounting Prac-
tice:Making the Right Choice," *Journal of Accountancy,*
February 1984, pp. 76–81.

Myers, Max, "Buying or Selling a Practice: Determining the Price,"
Taxation for Accountants, July 1972, pp. 63,64.

Smith, Houston D., "Valuing the Goodwill of a Local Practice Unit,"
CPA Practitioner, October 1978, pp. 1–2.

Torres, Paul D , "The Valuation of Professional Accounting Practices
–Guidelines for Buyers and Sellers," *National Public Accountant*, April 1978, pp. 24, 29–32.

Books and Pamphlets

Annual Statement Studies, Robert Morris Associates, Philadelphia, 1986.

Almanac of Business and Industrial Financial Ratios, Prentice-Hall, Englewood Cliffs, N.J., 1986.

Income and Fees of Accountants in Public Practice, National Society of Public Accountants, Alexandria, (no date).

Trade Journals

Accounting Education News
American Accounting Association
5717 Bessie Drive
Sarasota, FL 33583
((813) 921–7747

Accounting Issues
Bear Stearns & Co.
55 Water Street
New York, NY 10041
(212) 952–5000

CPA Journal
New York State Society of
Certified Public Accountants
600 Third Street
New York, NY 10016
(212) 661–2020

Journal of Accountancy
American Institute of Certified
Public Accountants
1221 Avenue of the Americas
New York, NY 10036-8775
(212) 575–6200

Journal of Accounting, Auditing & Finance
Warren, Gorham & Lamont
210 South Street
Boston, MA 02111
(617) 423–2020

National Public Accountant
National Society of
Public Accountants
1010 North Fairfax Street
Alexandria, VA 22314
(703) 549–6400

Practical Accountant
Warren, Gorham & Lamont
1633 Broadway
New York, NY 10019
(212) 971–5000

Taxation for Accountants
Warren, Gorham & Lamont
210 South Street
Boston, MA 02111
(617) 423–2020

3

Apparel Stores

Business Description   (SIC No. 5611-5699)

Apparel stores primarily engage in the retail sale of new clothing, shoes, hats, underwear, and related articles of personal wear and adornment.

Valuation Formulas

Two formulas are widely used to estimate the value of apparel stores, one based on a multiple of monthly net sales and the other on net operating profit.

Monthly Net Sales Formula

The monthly net sales formula is based on a multiple of average monthly net sales. The multiplier generally ranges from 2 to 7, with 4 to 5 being typical. The multiplier indicates a value for the trade fixtures, leasehold improvements, and intangible assets of the store.

Net Operating Profit Formula

The net operating profit formula applies a multiplier to the most recent 12 months of net profit, after reasonable compensation to the owner. Multipliers generally range from .75 to 1.5, with 1.0 being typical. This formula results in a value for intangible assets only. Fixed assets, such as trade fixtures and leasehold improvements, must be restated at market value and added to the formula value.

Net Equity Value

To estimate equity value, the value of net current assets, restated at market values less liabilities, is added to the value indicated by the multiplier.

Valuation Considerations

Among the variables considered in valuing an apparel shop are location, competition, reputation, specialization, and lease terms.

Location

Because location can be the major determining factor in the success of an apparel shop, it should be carefully scrutinized by the valuator. The following questions should be asked.

1. Does the store cater to the tastes of the surrounding community?
2. What are the area's shopping and growth patterns?
3. How much competition, if any, is there in the area?
4. Does the site have proximate, adequate parking? Is it accessible to pedestrians? Is it highly visible?
5. Does the street or shopping center need structural repairs? Is the immediate area in need of renovation? Is redevelopment planned for the area?
6. Is the store located in a high crime area where security is a problem?

Favorable answers to the above questions would indicate the use of a multiplier in the high end of the range.

Reputation

Because the value of the business goodwill is closely tied to the established clientele, the store's reputation with its customers should be considered. Does the store consistently buy quality, up-to-date merchandise? How personal is the service? What percentage of sales are from repeat business?

Specialization

There are many different types of specialized apparel stores, such as women's dress shops, shoe stores, and uniform shops. If the subject store specializes in one particular type of apparel or accessory line, the valuator should examine the individual market and specific factors related to that specialization. Such information can be obtained by contacting the national trade associations for specialized apparel retailers.

Lease Terms

In valuing apparel stores, careful attention must be paid to lease terms. The following items are important to consider with regard to lease arrangements: remaining time on the lease, renewal options, contract rent, right to sublease, and lessee responsibility for utilities and other expenses.

Retail apparel stores normally pay a flat rental rate calling for a set monthly amount, or they have a percentage-of-sales agreement with a minimum annual rent (commonly used by shopping centers). Percentage rents typically average 7 percent to 8 percent of gross sales but could be as high as 10 percent or even higher. In addition, there are often add-ons for parking lot maintenance, center advertising, or even local city fees. A percentage rental rate above 10 percent is considered unfavorable and would indicate a multiplier in the lower end of the range. A long-term lease with favorable terms may add considerably to the value of an apparel store.

Example

Step 1: Review and make a comparative analysis of income and expense for the previous three years.

Income and Expense Summary
for 12 months ending June 30

	19x6	19x7	19x8
Net Sales	$378,992	$395,432	$426,758
Cost of Sales	202,185	217,214	221,102
Gross Profit	176,807	178,218	205,656
Operating Expenses	132,699	134,565	142,063
Net Operating Profit*	$ 44,108	$ 43,653	$ 63,593

* Depreciation, excessive owner compensation and interest added back.

Note: It is important to consider income and expense trends as well as the current year's (19x8) data. To more accurately predict future economic trends, the valuator should review the most recent five years of financial data.

Step 2: Adjust the balance sheet to reflect the market value of tangible assets.

Balance Sheet Summary
as of June 30

	19x6	19x7	19x8	Restated at Market Value on Value Date
Assets				
Current Assets:				
Cash	$ 14,758	$ 16,488	$ 20,521	$ 20,521
Inventory	58,332	59,996	63,009	63,009
Total Current Assets	73,090	76,484	83,530	83,530
Fixed Assets:				
Trade Fixtures,				
Leasehold Improvements,				
and Equipment (net)	23,440	26,211	25,100	40,850
Total Assets	96,530	102,695	108,630	124,380
Liabilities	41,969	44,650	47,230	47,230
Net Tangible Equity	$ 54,561	$ 58,045	$ 61,400	$ 77,150

Example 27

Step 3: Apply the formulas.

Formula Valuation Using Monthly Net Sales Multiplier

Net Sales (Fiscal year end 6/30/x8)	$426,758
divided by 12	÷____12
Monthly Net Sales	35,563
Monthly Multiplier	×_____4
Indicated Gross Value of Fixed Assets and Intangibles	142,252
Plus Adjusted Market Value of Current Assets	83,530
Total Gross Value	225,782
Less Liabilities	47,230
Net Equity Value	$178,552

Formula Valuation Using Net Operating Profit Multiplier

Net Operating Profit (Fiscal year end 6/30/x8)	$ 63,593
Annual Multiplier	×___1.00
Indicated Value of Intangible Assets	63,593
Plus Adjusted Market Value of Tangible Assets	
Current	83,530
Fixed	40,850
Total Gross Value	187,973
Less Liabilities	47,230
Net Equity Value	$140,743

Sources of Further Information

Associations

American Apparel
Manufacturers Association
2500 Wilson Blvd., Suite 301
Arlington, VA 22201
(703) 524–1864

Menswear Retailers
of America
2011 I Street, N.W.
Washington, DC 20006
(202) 347–1932

Apparel Guild
Gallery 34, Suite 407
147 West 33rd Street
New York, NY 10001
(212) 279–4580

National Retail
Merchants Association
100 West 31st Street
New York, NY 10001
(212) 244–8780

Publications

Books and Pamphlets

Almanac of Business and Industrial Financial Ratios, Prentice-Hall,
Englewood Cliffs, N.J., 1986.

*Annual Statement Studie*s, Robert Morris Associates, Philadelphia,
1986.

*Apparel Stor*e, Starting Out Series, No. 122, U.S. Small Business Administration, Washington, D.C., September 1980.

Trade Journals

Bulletin
Menswear Retailers of America
2011 I Street N.W.
Washington, DC 20006
(202) 347–1932

Earnshaw's Infants,
Girls & Boys Review
Earnshaw Publications Inc.
393 Seventh Avenue
New York, NY 10001
(212) 563–2742

Daily News Record
Fairchild Publications Inc.
7 East 12th Street
New York, NY 10001
(212) 741–4000

Men's Wear
7 East 12th Street
New York, NY 10001
(212) 741–4000

Stores
National Retail
Merchants Association
100 West 31st Street
New York, NY 10001
(212) 244–8780

Teens' and Boys' Magazine
71 West 35th Street
New York, NY 10001
(212) 549–0880

Women's Wear Daily
Fairchild Publications Inc.
7 East 12th Street
New York, NY 10001
(212) 741–4000

4

Auto Body Repair and Paint Shops

Business Description (SIC No. 7531)

Auto body repair and paint shops primarily engage in the repair and painting of automobile bodies.

Valuation Formulas

Within the auto body industry, two market-derived formulas commonly are used in valuing body repair and paint shops. They are based on multiples of monthly net sales and net operating profit.

Monthly Net Sales Formula

The monthly net sales formula uses monthly net sales averaged over a specific period (usually the most recent 12 months). This revenue amount is most commonly multiplied by a factor ranging between 2 and 5, although monthly sales multipliers of 6 or 7 are not uncommon. The resulting value is specifically for fixed assets, such as trade equipment, and intangible assets, including goodwill. Multipliers in the high end of the range tend to be applied to auto body shops with longevity, a significant customer list, and good working relations with insurance agencies. (The same formula applies to auto mechanical repair, although the multiplier range is slightly lower, primarily because of higher exposure to potential liability and the presence of warranties.)

Auto Repair (NET) 2-6

Net Operating Profit Approach

The net operating profit approach applies a multiple of between 1 and 2 (1.5 being typical) to the net operating profit from the most recent 12-month period. The value indicated is specifically for intangible assets. Fixed assets should be restated at market value and added to the indicated value.

Net Equity Value

To estimate equity value, the value of net current assets, restated at market values less liabilities, is added to the value indicated by the use of the multiplier.

Valuation Considerations

Factors to consider when valuing an auto body repair and paint shop include the type of shop, its reputation and referral sources, the condition of its facilities and equipment, its location, and the lease terms.

Type of Shop

Auto body shops can be broken down into three major categories. At the bottom are low-priced shops with a minimum of body-working equipment, inexpensive or no frame-straightening equipment, and an inexpensive paint booth. These shops often contract out the frame straightening and major body work.

The second group usually repair all makes and models of automobiles. Their body and frame-straightening equipment can be adapted to most makes of vehicles, and they have one or two paint booths. Their personnel are experienced in most areas of body work.

At the top of the line are specialty shops. These shops specialize in certain makes or models of automobiles. The specialty may be general, such as sports cars, German cars, European cars, or Japanese cars, or may be more specific, such as Honda, Volvo, or Mercedes. They have specialized equipment for the makes and/or models they handle, charge top dollar, and their appearance draws the type of customer and product they service. Specialization may have a significant impact on the fee structure, percent of repeat business, and client base. It is important to evaluate the workmanship and facility as related to these factors.

Reputation and Referral Sources

Typically, the owner or owners have a great deal to do with the reputation and quality of the auto body repair and paint shop. They often are the final inspectors of the finished product and decide whether or not it is ready for the customer. The owner's years of experience may determine the shop's reputation. The loss of the owner upon sale of the business may have a significant impact on future operations and on the real value of the business. The tangible assets and location of the business may not be as important as the quality of management and the reputation the shop has developed under the present owner. If this is the case, there may be limited transferable goodwill unless the present owner agrees to stay with the shop for a period of time to ease the transfer to a new owner.

The owner may also be the reason for repeat business and maintenance of relations with referral sources. Referral sources and percent of repeat business may be the best measure of future revenue potential. This, however, depends on the probability of the owner assisting in the transfer of the business. Insurance companies, tow truck companies, car dealers, and credit institutions have contracts with and contacts in body shops. If the contracts can be transferred to a new owner, they may add considerably to the value of the business. Answers to the following questions will help in evaluating referral sources.

1.   What percentage of business is walk-in as opposed to personal referral? As opposed to insurance company referral?
2.   Does the shop have any existing contracts with either an insurance company or a rental car agency? Are such contracts based on the reputation of the owner?
3.   What is the referral spread and how loyal are the sources?

A body shop which receives a large percentage of its business from one referral source will have a greater risk of decreased future revenues.

Condition of Facilities and Equipment

The adequacy of the existing facility and equipment for both present and future needs should be assessed. Repair equipment is expensive and can represent a significant portion of the total outlay to open a new auto body shop. It is important, therefore, to evaluate whether or not there is any evidence of obsolescence. A shop with inadequate or obsolete equipment would receive a multiplier in the lower end of the range. If a great deal of renovation and modernization of the facility is required immediately, the multiplier should be lowered further.

Location

The location of the business and the area it has traditionally serviced is the last factor to be considered. Location probably dictates the type of body shop that is being operated. Better shops are usually located in better neighborhoods. It may be difficult to upgrade a business in a rundown or depressed area. A prime location would typically be on a well-traveled major traffic artery with good visibility. However, location may be secondary to reputation.

Lease Terms

In valuing any small business, consideration should be given to the existing lease terms. The following items are important to consider in regard to lease arrangements: amount of monthly rent, right to sublease, and responsibility for utilities and other expenses. A long-term lease with an option to renew would add considerably to the value of a shop.

Example 35

Example

Step 1: Review and make a comparative analysis of income and expense for the previous three years.

Income and Expense Summary
for 12 months ending June 30

	19x6	19x7	19x8
Net Sales	$389,932	$398,332	$441,224
Operating Expenses	360,215	366,212	404,048
Operating Profit*	$ 29,717	$ 32,120	$ 37,176

* Depreciation, excessive owner compensation, and interest added back.

Note: It is important to consider income and expense trends as well as the current year's (19x8) data. To more accurately predict future economic trends, the valuator should review the most recent five years of financial data.

Step 2: Adjust the balance sheet to reflect the market value of tangible assets.

Balance Sheet Summary
as of June 30

	19x6	19x7	19x8	Restated at Market Value on Value Date
Assets				
Current Assets:				
Cash	$ 8,568	$ 10,918	$ 17,431	$ 17,431
Receivables	34,748	38,945	40,008	38,600
Inventory	3,232	7,339	8,956	7,550
Total Current Assets	46,548	57,202	66,395	63,581
Fixed Assets:				
Trade Fixtures,				
Leasehold Improvements,				
and Equipment (net)	53,940	40,211	55,750	61,500
Total Assets	100,488	97,413	122,145	125,081
Liabilities	35,969	34,650	42,230	42,230
Net Tangible Equity	$ 64,519	$ 62,763	$ 79,915	$ 82,851

Step 3: Apply the formulas.

Formula Valuation Using Monthly Net Sales Multiplier

Net Sales (Fiscal year end 6/30/x8)	$441,224
divided by 12	÷ 12
Monthly Net Sales	36,769
Monthly Multiplier	× 3
Indicated Value of Fixed Assets and Intangibles	110,307
Plus Adjusted Market Value of Current Assets	63,581
Total Gross Value	173,888
Less Liabilities	42,230
Net Equity Value	$131,658

Formula Valuation Using Net Operating Profit Multiplier

Net Operating Profit (Fiscal year end 6/30/x8)	$ 37,176
Multiplier	× 1.5
Indicated Value of Intangibles	55,764
Plus Adjusted Market Value of Tangible Assets	
Current	63,581
Fixed	61,500
Total Gross	180,845
Less Liabilities	42,230
Net Equity Value	$138,615

Sources of Further Information

Associations

Automotive Information Council
29200 Southfield Road, Suite 111
Southfield, MI 48076
(313) 559–5922

Automotive Service Association
P.O. Box 929
Bedford, TX 76021
(817) 283–6205

Automotive Service Industry
Association
444 North Michigan Avenue
Chicago, IL 60611
(312) 836–1300

Inter-industry Conference
on Auto Collision Repair
2600 River Road #303
Des Plaines, IL 60018
(312) 699–1670

Motor and Equipment
Manufacturer Association
300 Sylvan Avenue
Englewood Cliff, NJ 07632
 (201) 569–8500

Society of Collision
Repair Specialists
1200 S. Outer Road
Blue Springs, MO 64015
(816) 228–6699

Publications

Books and Pamphlets

Almanac of Business and Industrial Financial Ratios, Prentice-Hall,
Englewood Cliffs, N.J., 1986.
Annual Statement Studies, Robert Morris Associates, Philadelphia,
1986.

Trade Journals

Auto Body Repair News
Stanley Publishing, Inc.
65 E. South Water Street,
20th Floor
Chicago, IL 60601
(312) 332–0210

Body Shop Business
Babcox Publishing, Inc.
11 South Forge Street
Acron, OH 44304
(216) 535–6117

5

Automobile Dealerships

Business Description   (SIC No. 5511)

Automobile dealerships primarily engage in the retail sale of new automobiles; they sometimes also sell used automobiles and frequently maintain repair departments and carry stocks of replacement parts, tires, batteries, and automotive accessories.

Valuation Formula

Valuation formulas for automobile dealerships are generally based on a multiple of the most current 12 months of annual net operating profit, plus the net tangible asset value. The multiplier generally ranges from 1 to 3, with 1.25 to 2 being typical. Operating profit multipliers at the higher end of the range are usually applied to dealerships with high earnings and a well-established reputation. These include high-ticket dealerships such as Mercedes-Benz and BMW. The multiplier is applied to the net operating profit from the adjusted 12-month statement, not from the dealer-to-factory 13-month statement. The use of the multiplier results in a value for the dealership's goodwill. Fixed assets, such as trade fixtures and equipment, must be added to the value indicated by the use of the multiplier.

Net Equity Value

To estimate equity value, the value of net current assets, restated at market values less liabilities, is added to the value resulting from the use of the multiplier. Net current assets include depreciable current assets at market value and the inventory of used cars (unless on consignment), parts, and accessories. The new car inventory is not included.

Valuation Considerations

Among the variables that must be considered in valuing an automobile dealership are type of dealership, location, economic climate, and the history and financial condition of the business, and lease terms.

Type of Dealership

Different types of dealerships have different values according to car make, marketability, and factory allocation. Historically, Japanese import dealerships have received higher multipliers than domestic dealerships. However, in recent years the gap has narrowed due to the upsurge in domestic model marketability and third-world competition. At present, multipliers are not determined so much by whether the dealership is foreign or domestic but rather by the quality and marketability of the product line, factory allocation policy, and whether the dealership is an exclusive or dual-point location. Factory allocation may be based on a number of factors such as area market share or number of cars sold.

A facility with dual points, which carries both an import and a domestic product line, might also command a multiplier at the high end of the range. This combination can lower the risk factors of tightened restrictions on foreign imports or a possible decrease in domestic marketability. To value a dual-point entity, the multiplier applicable to the more highly valued dealership should be applied to the entire entity.

Location

The location of the dealership may also greatly affect the multiplier. Facilities located on an automobile row or in an auto shopping mall with "constructive competition" are extremely attractive and can be highly profitable. Demographic trends and market share in the surrounding area should also be reviewed to analyze profit potential.

Multipliers can also be affected by regional differences. Dealerships in the Sunbelt often receive higher multipliers than dealerships in the Northwest. Domestic dealerships tend to control a larger market share in the Midwest than in many other regions and could command higher multipliers than import sellers in the same area. Because automobile sales mirror general business conditions and closely reflect changes in disposable personal income, regional economic conditions must be reviewed at the time of valuation to gain an accurate picture of profit potential.

History and Financial Condition

The history and financial condition of the business in question should be reviewed, as well as the owner's records on sales and service. Longevity and reputation of the operation, employee turnover rate, and pending obligations (such as contracts and warranties) may have an effect on the multiplier.

Lease Terms

In valuing any small business, consideration should be given to the existing lease terms. Important items to consider in regard to lease arrangements are amount of monthly rent, right to sublease, and lessee responsibility for utilities and other expenses. A long-term lease with an option to renew would substantially increase the value of a dealership.

Example

Step 1: Review and make a comparative analysis of income an expense for the last three years.

Income and Expense Summary
for 12 months ending June 30

	19x6	19x7	19x8
Total Sales	$7,710,594	$9,334,735	$10,476,167
Cost of Cars	6,651,929	8,075,476	8,979,123
Gross Profit	1,058,665	1,259,259	1,497,044
Net Operating Expenses	893,659	1,055,758	1,266,569
Net Operating Profit*	$ 165,006	$ 203,501	$ 203,475

* Depreciation, excessive owner compensation, and interest added back.

Note: It is important to consider income and expense trends, as well as the current year's (19x8) data. To more accurately predict future economic trends, the valuator should review the most recent five years of financial data.

Step 2: Adjust the balance sheet to reflect the market value of tangible assets.

Balance Sheet Summary
as of June 30

	19x6	19x7	19x8	Restated at Market Value on Value Date
Assets				
Current Assets:				
Cash	$ 87,943	$ 98,746	$103,450	$103,450
Accounts Receivable	131,317	120,042	124,285	116,725
Inventory	277,040	275,156	310,940	310,940
Total Current Assets	496,300	493,944	538,675	531,115
Fixed Assets:				
Furniture, Fixtures,				
Leasehold Improvements				
and Equipment (net)	75,539	79,648	76,908	93,300
Total Assets	571,839	573,592	615,583	624,415
Liabilities	258,396	249,223	245,335	245,335
Net Tangible Equity	$313,443	$324,369	$370,248	$379,080

Example 43

Step 3: Apply the formula.

Formula Valuation Using Net Operating Profit Multiplier

Net Operating Profit (Fiscal year end 6/30/x8)	$203,475
Annual Multiplier	×_____2
Indicated Value of Intangibles	406,950
Plus Adjusted Market Value of Assets	
Current	531,115
Fixed	93,300
Total Gross Value	1,031,365
Less Liabilities	245,335
Net Equity Value	$ 786,030

Sources of Further Information

Associations

American Automobile Association
8111 Gatehouse Road
Falls Church, VA 22047
(703) 222–6000

Dealers' Alliance
401 Hackensack
Hackensack, NJ 07601
(201) 342–4542

American International
Auto Dealers' Association
1128 16th Street , N.W.
Washington, DC 20036
(202) 659–2561

National Automobile
Dealers' Association
8400 West park Drive
McLean, VA 22102
(703) 821–7000

Publications

Books and Pamphlets

Almanac of Business and Industrial Financial Ratios, Prentice-Hall, Englewood Cliffs, N.J., 1986.
Annual Statement Studies, Robert Morris Associates, Philadelphia, 1986.
West, Elmer H., *How to Sell A Dealership,* Exposition Press, New York, 1980.

Trade Magazines

Auto Age
Freed, Crown & Royal Publishers
6931 Van Nuys Blvd.
Van Nuys, CA 91405
(818) 997–0644

Automotive News
Crain Communications, Inc.
1400 Woodbridge
Detroit, MI 48207
(313) 446–6000

Automotive Executive
National Automobile Dealers' Association
8400 Westpark Drive
McLean, VA 22102
(703) 821–7000

6

Auto Parts Retailers and Jobbers

Business Description (SIC No. 5531)

Auto parts retailers and jobbers primarily engage in the retail sale and wholesale of automobile parts and accessories.

Valuation Formula

Auto parts retailers and jobbers typically sell for a very limited goodwill premium over the net asset value. This is due primarily to the ease of entry into the marketplace and the asset-intensive nature of the business. The small premium that may be paid for an auto parts dealer depends on the following factors:

— Expected price increase imposed by distributor or manufacturer
— Furniture and fixtures depreciated to less than 35 percent of their original cost
— Low interest rates (In periods of low interest rates, it is not uncommon for jobbers to receive substantial premiums over book value. If interest rates are high, there may be no premium applied to the business value.)
— Exceptional location
— Leasehold interest

Given the above factors, the intangible value of a retailer or jobber would be a multiple of annual net operating profit. Multipliers generally range anywhere from .25 to 1.0. The market value of fixed

45

assets, such as trade fixtures and equipment, should be added to the value of the intangible assets.

Net Equity Value

In order to value the total business equity, current assets, including cash, inventory, and accounts receivable should be restated at market value and added to the intangible and fixed asset value. Liabilities to be assumed should then be deducted.

Valuation Considerations

Variables that should be considered when valuing an auto parts retailer or jobber include location, inventory, supplier relations, and lease terms.

Location

As previously stated, the existence of intangible value for auto parts retailers and jobbers is partially dependant on location. The following factors are essential to investigate in regard to location.

1. *Vehicle Registration.* The number of vehicles registered with the Department of Motor Vehicles indicates the market size of a given area.
2. *Customer Potential.* The number of customer outlets must be determined. If the subject store is primarily a wholesaler, check the number of service stations, garages and repair shops in the surrounding area. If the business is primarily a retail shop, the number of homes and apartment units surrounding the site indicate customer potential. A check into the number and types of competing stores will help determine the market share for any single business.
3. *Parking.* The very nature of an auto supply store requires convenient parking. The number and location of off-street parking facilities is important because customers drive vehicles in to obtain necessary parts. Accessibility to the parking area must also be considered.

4. *Traffic Count.* Traffic count is especially important for locations within a large metropolitan area where commuter traffic boosts sales. In many cities, car dealers and auto repair shops tend to concentrate in one geographic area, and proximity to these auto centers makes selling to the trade easier.

Inventory

Available inventory, cost, and turnover rate are the most valuable elements to a retailer's or jobber's sales volume and value. The difference between what the store owner pays for the inventory at cost and what it is sold for at retail or wholesale is termed the gross profit margin. Typical gross profit margins for auto parts stores are: retail, 30 percent to 45 percent; wholesale, 25 percent to 33 1/3 percent; combination, 30 percent to 40 percent.

Inventory turnover is the key to profits. Auto parts merchants report turnover rates ranging from 2 to 5, with an average of 3.1. Higher inventory turnover rates of 4 to 5 generally indicate less obsolescence and computer control of the inventory. Inventory turnover ratios of 4 to 5 are not uncommon in sole-source establishments such as NADA, where inventory buy back of obsolete items and central computer control are part of the services offered. High inventory turnover may be a sign of potential intangible value.

Supplier Relations

Many retailers and jobbers have sole-source relationships with suppliers. The established relationship with the shop's main suppliers as well as the programs offered by the suppliers should be examined since they are an asset to the business. Manufacturer and distributor policies and programs such as financial help on expansion orders, comprehensive obsolescence protection, and seasonal advertising programs all contribute to the success of the individual retailer or jobber. Some suppliers even offer management training courses and automatic ordering. This can aid the retailer or jobber in decreasing costs and increasing inventory turnover rate.

Further, the supplier's priority in order fulfillment is often based on longevity of association and is a valuable intangible asset for an auto parts shop. If the shop owner has nurtured these relationships and made use of the supplier's programs, it is likely to add to the value of the business.

Lease Terms

In valuing any small business, consideration should be given to the existing lease terms. The following items are important to consider in regard to lease arrangements: amount of monthly rent, right to sublease, and responsibility for utilities and other expenses. A long-term lease with an option to renew would add considerably to the value of a jobber.

Example 49

Example

Step 1: Review and make a comparative analysis of income and expense for the previous three years.

Income and Expense Summary
for 12 months ending June 30

	19x6	19x7	19x8
Net Revenue	$750,475	$775,040	$801,324
Cost of Sales	477,501	493,750	510,273
Gross Profit	272,974	281,290	291,051
Operating Expenses	220,128	227,086	234,113
Net Operating Profit*	$ 52,846	$ 54,204	$ 56,938

* Depreciation, excessive owner compensation, and interest added back.

Note: It is important to consider income and expense trends as well as the current year's (19x8) data. To more accurately predict future economic trends, the valuator should review the most recent five years of financial data.

Step 2: Adjust the balance sheet to reflect the market value of tangible assets.

Balance Sheet Summary
as of June 30

	19x6	19x7	19x8	Restated at Market Value on Value Date
Assets				
Current Assets:				
Cash	$ 27,890	$ 32,111	$ 34,897	$ 34,897
Accounts Receivable	31,980	37,251	39,788	38,450
Inventory	120,000	125,000	130,000	125,000
Total Current Assets	179,870	194,362	204,685	198,347
Fixed Assets:				
Trade Fixtures & Equipment	71,858	64,746	57,978	75,000
Total Assets	251,728	259,108	262,663	273,347
Liabilities	89,258	85,621	81,773	81,773
Net Tangible Equity	$162,470	$173,487	$180,890	$191,574

Step 3: Apply the formula.

Formula Valuation Using Net Operating Profit

Net Operating Profit (Fiscal year end 06/30/x8)	$ 56,938
Multiplier	×___.75
Indicated Value of Intangible Assets	42,704
Plus Adjusted Market Value of Assets	
Current	198,347
Fixed	75,000
Total Gross Value	316,051
Less Liabilities	81,773
Net Equity Value	$234,278

Sources of Further Information

Associations

Automotive Information Council
29200 Southfield Road, #111
Southfield, MI 48076
(313) 559–5922

Automotive Parts and
Accessories Association
5100 Forbes Boulevard
Lanham, MD 20706
(301) 459–9110

Automotive Service
Industry Association
444 North Michigan Avenue
Chicago, IL 60611
(312) 836–1300

Motor and Equipment
Manufacturers' Association
300 Sylvan Avenue
P.O. Box 1638
Englewood Cliff, NJ 07632
(201) 569–8500

Publications

Books and Pamphlets

Almanac of Business and Industrial Financial Ratios, Prentice-Hall,
    Englewood Cliffs, N.J., 1986.
Annual Statement Studies, Robert Morris Associates, Philadelphia,
    1986.
Auto Supply Stores, Bank of America–Small Business Reporter, San
    Francisco,1979.

Trade Journals

Aftermarket Business
Harcourt Brace
Jovanovich Publications
7500 Old Oak Boulevard
Cleveland, OH 44130
(216) 243–8100

Automotive Aftermarket News
Stanley Publishing
65 East Wacker Place, 20th Floor
Chicago, IL 60601
(312) 332–0210

Automotive Marketing
Chilton Company
201 King of Prussia Road
Radnor, PA 19089
(215) 964–4000

Jobber Retail Magazine
Bill Communications
110 North Miller Road
Acron, OH 44313
(216) 867–4401

Jobber Topics
The Irving-Cloud
Publishing Company
7300 North Cicelo
Linconwood, IL 60646
(312) 588–7300

7

Beauty Salons

Business Description   (SIC No. 7231)

Beauty salons primarily engage in furnishing hair care services. This industry also includes combination beauty and barber shops.

Valuation Formula

The industry recognizes two market-derived formulas that are useful in the valuation of beauty salons. These formulas are based on multiples of monthly net revenue and net operating profit.

Monthly Net Revenue Formula

The monthly net revenue formula applies a multiple to the average monthly net revenue from the latest 12-month period. Multiplier commonly range from 3 to 5, with 4 being typical. The value resulting from the use of the formula is for fixed assets, such as trade fixtures and equipment, and intangible assets, such as goodwill.

Net Operating Profit Formula

The net operating profit formula applies a multiple ranging from 1.5 to 3 to the net profit from the latest 12-month period, with 2 to 2.5 being typical. If the last 12 months cannot be considered normal, an average of the last 24 or 36 months may be used. The value resulting from the use of the formula is for fixed and intangible assets.

Net Equity Value

In order to value the net business equity, current assets including cash, inventory, and accounts receivable should be restated at market value and added to the value indicated by the use of the formulas. Liabilities should then be deducted.

Valuation Considerations

Variables that should be considered when estimating the value of a beauty salon include transferability, location, clientele characteristics, diversification of sales and services, and current lease terms.

Transferability

The value of a beauty salon depends primarily on its ability to obtain and retain clients. In this type of personal service business, the personality and skill of the owner and the individual stylists are of paramount importance. According to one industry expert, the average client attrition rate is between 10 percent and 15 percent during a typical year. However, upon the sale of the salon, client attrition is often very high (up to 50 percent). This makes salons extremely difficult to sell. It is therefore imperative that the ease of transferability and probable retention of the client base be analyzed. Client retention is inexplicably linked to staff retention, and it is recommended that a potential buyer interview each individual stylist.

If the salon owner rents out stations to independent stylists rather than employing a full-time staff, the probability of both client and stylist attrition is further increased. Independent stylists tend to have a high turnover rate, often taking clients with them. If the beauty salon would be unable to retain its patrons after the transfer, the business would have little intangible value.

Location

In an analysis of the subject location, visibility as well as accessibility and traffic count must be examined. The site should be on a main traffic artery or at least on a heavily traveled secondary route. Shopping mall locations can also be successful because of the high volume of foot traffic.

The valuator should examine the neighborhood in order to determine the extent to which the establishment matches the community environment. Location often dictates the makeup of the client base as well as the fee structure. Demographic variables of the surrounding community such as age and sex distribution and average household income should be examined in order to predict future revenue potential and associated risk factors.

According to the National Hairdressers and Cosmetologists Association, 51 percent of all women over 45 visit a beauty salon in a four-week period, as opposed to 27 percent of women between the ages of 18 and 45. Obviously, a salon located in an older, family-oriented community would tend to have a larger untapped market potential than one in a more transient younger community.

Client Characteristics

An analysis of the characteristics of the salon's clientele is important in formulating a realistic assessment of stability and revenue potential. The following questions should be answered in an examination of the client base.

1. What is the average client age?
2. How often does the average client visit the salon?
3. What percentage of the clientele have low maintenance hair cuts?
4. What is the average expenditure per client visit?
5. How many clients have weekly standing appointments?
6. What is the average longevity of the clients?

Favorable answers to the above questions would indicate the appropriateness of a multiplier in the higher end of the range.

Diversification of Sales

Due to the high commissions often paid to stylists (typically 55 percent of sales), many salons find it is necessary to increase their gross revenue and profit margin by diversifying into retail sales, nail and skin care, and tanning services. Additional services such as these help obtain and retain clients. Some services, such as tanning, have high profit margins and help supplement hair care revenues. Retail sales have a particularly high gross profit margin, often reaching as high as 100 percent.

The diversification of hair care services should also be examined. Different services have different gross profit margins and turnover rates. Chemical services, such as color rinses and permanents, have by far the highest profit margins. What percent of revenues is attributed to such services? Is the subject salon making the most of its profit potential or is there room for improvement?

Lease Terms

In valuing any small business, consideration should be given to the existing lease terms for the real property. Important items to consider in analyzing lease arrangements are: the amount of monthly rent, the right to sublease, and the responsibility for maintenance, taxes, insurance, and other property expenses. A long-term lease with an option to renew would add considerably to the value of a beauty salon.

Example 57

Example

Step 1: Review and make a comparative analysis of income and expense for the previous three years.

Income and Expense Summary
for 12 months ending June 30

	19x6	19x7	19x8
Net Revenue	$163,058	$169,218	$176,345
Operating Expenses	138,220	142,988	149,092
Net Operating Profit*	$ 24,838	$ 26,230	$ 27,253

* Depreciation, excessive owner compensation, and interest added back.

Note: It is important to consider income and expense trends as well as the current year's (19x8) data. To more accurately predict future economic trends, the valuator should review the most recent five years of financial data.

Step 2: Adjust the balance sheet to reflect the market value of tangible assets.

Balance Sheet Summary
as of June 30

	19x6	19x7	19x8	Restated at Market Value on Value Date
Assets				
Current Assets:				
Cash	$ 7,361	$ 6,500	$ 7,139	$ 7,139
Inventory	587	523	625	585
Total Current Assets	7,948	7,023	7,764	7,724
Fixed Assets:				
Trade Fixtures,				
Leasehold Improvements,				
and Equipment	20,108	16,311	12,001	13,775
Total Assets	28,056	23,334	19,765	21,499
Liabilities	11,291	9,825	7,210	7,210
Net Tangible Equity	$16,765	$13,509	$12,555	$14,289

Step 3: Apply the formulas.

Formula Valuation Using Average Monthly Net Sales

Annual Net Revenue(Fiscal year end 6/30/x8)	$176,345
divided by 12	÷ 12
Average Monthly Net Revenue	14,695
Multiplier	× 4
Indicated Value of Fixed Assets and Intangibles	$ 58,780
Plus Adjusted Market Value of Current Assets	7,724
Total Gross Value	66,504
Less Liabilities	7,210
Net Equity Value	$59,294

Formula Valuation Using Net Operating Profit

Net Operating Profit (Fiscal year end 06/30/x8)	$ 27,253
Multiplier	× 2.25
Indicated Value of Fixed Assets and Intangibles	61,319
Plus Adjusted Market Value of Current Assets	7,724
Total Gross Value	69,043
Less Liabilities	7,210
Net Equity Value	$ 61,833

Sources of Further Information

Associations

National Beauty Salon
Chain Association
610 South Main Avenue
High Point, NC 27260
(605) 336–7080

National Hairdresser's and
Cosmetologist's Association
3510 Olive Street
St. Louis, MO 63103
(314) 534–7980

Publications

Books and Pamphlets

Almanac of Business and Industrial Financial Ratios, Prentice-Hall,
Englewood Cliffs, N.J.,1986.
Annual Statement Studies, Robert Morris Associates, Philadelphia,
1986.

Articles

Anderson, Howard. "Selling Your Salon," *Cutter Magazine,*
February 1981, pp. 11–14.
"Fatal Flaws," *Cutter Magazine*, November 1986, p. 13.
"How to Sell Your Salon: A Six-Step Guide," *Cutter Magazine,*
March 1986, p. 15.
"What Affects Your Salon's Value?" *Cutter Magazine,* December
1986, p. 16.
"What is Your Salon Worth?" *Cutter Magazine,* March 1986, pp. 14–
15.

Trade Journals

American Salon Magazine
Harcourt Brace
Jovanovich Publications
7500 Old Oak Boulevard
Cleveland, OH 44130
(216) 243–8100

Cutter Magazine
Whale Publishing Group, Inc.
183 Route 81
Killingworth, CT 06417
(203) 663–2991

Modern Salon Magazine
Vance Publishing Corporation
P.O. Box 400
Prairie View, IL 60069
(312) 634–2600

8

Bicycle Shops

Business Description (SIC No. 5941)

Bicycle shops primarily engage in the retail sale of bicycles, bicycle parts, accessories, and repairs.

Valuation Formula

Valuation formulas for bicycle shops are based on a multiple of average monthly net sales. The multiplier generally ranges from 3 to 5. The value indicated by the use of the multiplier is specifically for trade fixtures, equipment, and intangible assets, such as goodwill.

Net Equity Value

To estimate equity value, the value of net current assets, restated at market values less liabilities, is added to the value indicated by the use of the multiplier.

Valuation Considerations

Among the factors that should be considered when selecting a multiplier are revenue mix, location, competition, and current lease terms.

Revenue Mix

Bicycle shops generally have three sources of revenue: new bike sales, sales of accessories and parts, and repairs. When using a net sales formula, it is important to review the percentage of sales attributable to each revenue source in relation to its gross profit margin. The gross profit margin for new bike sales ranges from 25 percent to 35 percent. Because of this low profit margin, most bicycle shops supplement sales of new bikes with sales of parts and accessories and repairs, all of which carry higher gross profit margins. A bike shop generally needs a revenue mix of approximately 50 percent new bike sales, 30 percent accessories and parts sales, and 20 percent repairs to be reasonably profitable. A shop whose parts and accessories sales and repairs are in excess of 50 percent of total revenue would warrant a multiplier in the higher end of the range.

Shops that specialize in professional bicycles tend to have a higher percentage of business attributable to parts, accessories, and repairs due to the sensitivity and precision of the bikes and their relatively high price.

Location

The market area for a bicycle shop tends to be within a five-mile radius of the location. An analysis of the area and location should consider the following questions.

1. What is the general income level of the customer base within the market area? (An average income level of at least $25,000 is necessary to support a bike shop.)
2. Does the area have a high concentration of single-family homes? Are any changes in the community structure foreseeable in the near future?
3. Does the life-style of the area promote exercise and outdoor recreation?
4. Is a significant portion of the population near retirement age? (Senior citizens tend to be the best market for exercise bikes, which have a high markup.)
5. Is the geographic region and climate conducive to bike sales? (Shops in the Southwest tend to be most profitable.)
6. Is the store located on a major traffic artery with good visibility and adjacent parking?

A bicycle shop with favorable answers to the above questions would tend to receive a multiplier in the high end of the range.

Competition

Competition, both expected and existing, must also be evaluated. Mass merchandising chain stores control 70 percent of the retail bicycle market and can be a serious threat to a small bike shop. All competing bike shops should be compared to the subject shop in relation to lines offered and degree of specialization.

Lease Terms

In valuing a bike shop consideration should be given to the existing lease terms. The following items should be considered in regard to lease arrangements: amount of monthly rent, right to sublease, and lessee responsibility for utilities and other expenses. A long-term lease with an option to renew would add considerably to the value of a bicycle shop.

Example

Step 1: Review and make a comparative analysis of income and expense for the previous three years.

Income and Expense Summary
for 12 months ending June 30

	19x6	19x7	19x8
Net Sales	$124,942	$158,934	$173,926
Cost of Sales	81,212	103,307	113,052
Gross Profit	43,730	55,627	60,874
Operating Expenses	38,732	49,269	53,917
Net Operating Profit*	$ 4,998	$ 6,358	$ 6,957

* Depreciation, excessive owner compensation, and interest added back.

Note: It is important to consider income and expense trends, as well as the current year's (19x8) data. To more accurately predict future economic trends, the valuator should review the most recent five years of financial data.

Step 2: Adjust the balance sheet to reflect the market value of tangible assets.

Balance Sheet Summary
as of June 30

	19x6	19x7	19x8	Restated at Market Value on Value Date
Assets				
Current Assets:				
Cash	$ 4,758	$ 5,488	$ 5,521	$ 5,521
Inventory	27,932	29,969	33,056	33,056
Total Current Assets	32,690	35,457	38,577	38,577
Fixed Assets:				
Trade Fixtures and Equipment (net)	9,440	10,211	9,750	10,500
Total Assets	42,130	45,668	48,327	49,077
Liabilities	5,969	5,650	7,230	7,230
Net Tangible Equity	$ 36,161	$ 40,018	$ 41,097	$ 41,847

Step 3: Apply the formula.

Formula Valuation Using Monthly Net Sales Multiplier

Net Sales (Fiscal year end 6/30/x8)	$173,926
divided by 12	÷ _____12
Monthly Gross Sales	14,494
Monthly Multiplier	×_____3
Indicated Value of Fixed Assets and Intangibles	43,482
Plus Adjusted Market Value of Current Assets	38,577
Total Gross Value	82,059
Less Liabilities	7,230
Net Equity Value	$ 74,829

Sources of Further Information

Associations

Bicycle Manufacturers'
Association of America, Inc.
1055 Thomas Jefferson, Suite 308
Washington, DC 20007
(202) 333–4052

Cycle Parts and
Accessories Association
122 East 42nd Street
New York, NY 101168
(212) 697–6340

Bicycle Wholesale
Distributors Association, Inc.
North Plaza Building
99 West Hawthorne Avenue
Valley Stream, NY 11580
(516) 825–3000

National Bicycle
Dealer's Association
P.O. Box 3450
Mission Viejo, CA 92690
(714) 951–3451

Publications

Books and Pamphlets

Almanac of Business and Industrial Financial Ratios, Prentice-Hall, Englewood Cliffs, N.J., 1986.

Annual Statement Studies, Robert Morris Associates, Philadelphia, 1986.

Bicycle Stores, Bank of America Small-Business Reporter, San Francisco, 1981.

Bicycles, Starting Out Series, No. 133, U.S. Small Business Administration, Washington, D.C., September 1980.

Trade Journals

*American Bicyclist
and Motorcyclist*
Cycling Press, Inc.
461 Eighth Avenue
New York, NY 10001
(212) 563–4834

Bicycle Journal
Quinn Publications, Inc.
P.O. Box 1570
Fort Worth, TX 76101
(800) 245–5946

Bicycle Dealer Showcase
Hester Communications Incorporated
P.O. Box 19531
Irvine, CA 92713
(714) 549–4834

BMX Plus!
BMX Plus! Publications, Inc.
20705 Western Avenue, #108
Torrance, CA 90501
(213) 533–7104

9

Bowling Centers

Business Description (SIC No. 7933)

Bowling centers are better known to the public as bowling alleys or lanes. Such establishments frequently sell meals and refreshments.

Valuation Formulas

The industry recognizes three market-derived formulas for ascertaining the total business value (including fixed and intangible assets), exclusive of real property, of a bowling center. They are based on multiples of annual net sales, net operating profit, and number of lanes.

Annual Net Sales Formula

The annual net sales formula uses the most recent 12 months of net sales, including revenue from a cocktail lounge, but excluding revenue from food sales. (Revenue from food sales should be included if the center operates a large sit-down restaurant that attracts nonbowlers or contracts out a snack bar operation and receives a percentage of the gross food sales.) The formula applies a multiple ranging from 1 to 1.5 to the resulting net sales figure.

The Net Operating Profit Formula

The net operating profit formula applies a multiplier ranging from 3 to 6, with 4 to 5 being typical, to the most recent 12 months of net operating profit. If the latest 12 months of net operating profit cannot be considered normal, an average of the last 24 to 36 months may be used.

Number of Lanes Formula

The number of lanes formula applies a dollar value to the number of bowling lanes available in the establishment. The dollar value range varies from $10,000 to $20,000 per lane. However, $12,500 to $15,000 is more typical. For example, using this formula the indicated value of a 32-lane bowling center would be $480,000 (32 x $15,000).

Net Equity Value

In order to value the total business equity, current assets including cash, inventory, and accounts receivable should be restated at market value and added to the value indicated by the use of the formula. Liabilities should then be deducted.

Valuation Considerations

Major factors that must be considered when valuing a bowling center include revenue per lane and lineage, location, customer base, supplemental income and the presence of a liquor license, condition of the lanes and bowling equipment, and current lease terms if the real estate is not owned.

Revenue per Lane and Lineage

Two rule-of-thumb checks useful in evaluating the financial health of a bowling center are revenue per lane and lineage. Revenue per lane is defined as the total revenue divided by the number of lanes present. A healthy center should have a revenue ratio of at least $20,000 to $25,000 per lane.

A second check refers to lineage. According to one industry expert, lineage is defined as the number of paid games per lane per year. The industry average for lineage is approximately 10,000 per lane annually. The financial health of a center with lineage substantially under 10,000 would be suspect. However, the accuracy of both of these checks is contingent on the other considerations discussed in this section.

Location

Location is one of the most important variables in the success of a bowling center. Most bowling centers service a market area within a fifteen- to twenty-mile radius from the subject business. In an analysis of the area and site, the following questions should be considered.

1. What are the current and projected population figures for the area? (The industry rule of thumb in determining what population base is necessary to operate profitably is roughly 1,000 to 1,200 potential bowlers per lane. For a 32-lane center, the market area should contain at least a population of 32,000, assuming there is no other direct competition in the area.)
2. Is the geographic region and economic climate conducive to the profitability of a bowling center? (Bowling centers in the Sunbelt tend to be more profitable due to a higher percentage of year round play and a lower level of competition than in the Midwest and East.)
3. Is the bowling center located on a major traffic artery? Is it easily accessible and visible from the street?
4. What is the quantity and quality of the competition in the area?

Favorable answers to the above questions would indicate the use of a multiplier in the high end of the range.

Customer Base

Another important consideration that should be examined when selecting a multiplier is the customer base makeup of regulars versus league bowlers. According to the National Bowling Association, a league bowler typically bowls an average of three times a week, thirty-six weeks of the year. Further, during the off season, the league bowler will continue to play more often than the recreational player. If a large percentage (at least 70–75 percent) of business is not derived from league bowling, the center may not have a stable customer base. If this is the case, the multiplier would be negatively affected.

Supplemental Income and Liquor License

According to industry statistics, 50 percent or more of the gross revenue should come from bowling in a well-run center; 33 percent from a cocktail lounge; and 17 percent from food sales and a pro shop. However, it is not uncommon for the revenue from an in-house bar operation to exceed these guidelines. Active and well-managed lounges often draw nonbowlers. Because of this, an on-premises beer and wine license and/or liquor license can greatly enhance the goodwill of a bowling alley due to the high profit margin on bar sales. The presence of either one of these licenses would have a positive effect on the multiplier.

Depending on state-imposed restrictions on transferability, a liquor license may develop a significant market value independent of the bowling center business. A thorough analysis of the licensing laws should be conducted, as they differ substantially from state to state. If the bowling center has a liquor license saleable in the market separately from the business, it should be restated at market value and added with the other current assets.

Condition of Lanes and Bowling Equipment

The adequacy of the existing facility for both present and future needs must be assessed. Factors that should be considered for a thorough analysis include

- the exterior image of the building
- the condition and energy efficiency of the major equipment, including pinspotter, automatic scorer, ball return, bowling lanes, control unit, gutters, kickback, masking panels, pin deck, and scoring ensemble
- the adequacy of the eating facility, cocktail lounge, cashier station, and public restrooms

The older and more obsolete the facility, the lower the multiplier. If a great deal of renovation and modernization is required immediately, the multiplier should be lowered further.

Lease Terms

In valuing any small business, consideration should be given to the existing lease terms for the real property. The following items should be considered in regard to such lease arrangements: amount of monthly rent, right to sublease and responsibility for utilities and other expenses. A long-term lease with an option to renew would add considerably to the value of a bowling center.

Example

Step 1: Review and make a comparative analysis of income and expense for the previous three years.

Income and Expense Summary
for 12 months ending June 30

	19x6	19x7	19x8
Net Sales:			
Bowling	$349,192	$363,987	$367,654
Bar	159,871	174,599	188,946
Food	89,772	96,271	99,944
Total Sales	598,835	634,857	656,562
Cost of Sales			
Bar	45,481	50,073	54,209
Food	34,821	41,424	42,075
Gross Profit	518,533	543,360	560,278
Operating Expenses	401,056	395,546	412,095
Net Operating Profit*	$117,477	$147,814	$148,183

* Depreciation, excessive owner compensation, and interest added back.

Note: It is important to consider income and expense trends as well as the current year's (19x8) data. To more accurately predict future economic trends, the valuator should review the most recent five years of financial data.

Step 2: Adjust the balance sheet to reflect the market value of tangible assets.

Balance Sheet Summary
as of June 30

	19x6	19x7	19x8	Restated at Market Value on Value Date
Current Assets	40,055	49,885	63,513	62,045
Fixed Assets	184,964	163,849	129,837	245,850
Total Assets	225,019	213,734	193,350	307,895
Liabilities	11,016	14,204	33,993	33,993
Net Tangible Equity	$214,003	$199,530	$159,357	$273,902

Example 75

Step 3: Apply the formulas.

Formula Valuation Using Annual Net Sales

Net Sales (Fiscal year end 6/30/x8)	$656,562
Less Food Sales	− 99,944
	556,618
Multiplier	× 1.0
Indicated Value of Fixed Assets and Intangibles	556,618
Plus Adjusted Market Value of Current Assets	62,045
Total Gross Value	618,663
Less Liabilities	33,993
Net Equity Value	$584,670

Formula Valuation Using Net Operating Profit

Net Operating Profit (Fiscal year end 6/30/x8)	$148,183
Multiplier	× 3.5
Indicated Value of Fixed Assets and Intangibles	518,641
Plus Adjusted Market Value of Current Assets	62,045
Total Gross Value	580,686
Less Liabilities	33,993
Net Equity Value	$546,693

Formula Valuation Using the Number of Lanes

Value Per Lane	$ 15,000
Number of Lanes	× 32
Indicated Value of Fixed Asset and Intangibles	480,000
Plus Adjusted Market Value of Current Assets	62,045
Total Gross Value	542,045
Less Liabilities	33,993
Net Equity Value	$508,052

Sources of Further Information

Associations

Billiard and Bowling
Institute of America
200 Castlewood Drive
North Palm Beach, FL 33408
(305) 842–4100

Bowling Proprietors'
Association of America
P.O. Box 5802
Arlington, TX 76011
(817) 649–5109

Distributors

AMS Bowling Company, Inc.
P.O. Box 31640
Colonnade at Innsbrook
4050 Inns Lake Drive
Richmond, Virginia 23294
(804) 747–6300

Brunswick Corporation
P.O. Box 329
525 West Laketon Avenue
Muskegon, MI 49443
(616) 726–3300

Publications

Books and Pamphlets

Almanac of Business and Industrial Financial Ratios, Prentice-Hall,
Englewood Cliffs, N.J., 1986.
Annual Statement Studies, Robert Morris Associates, Philadelphia,
1986.
Bowling Center (AEA Business Manual No. X1269), American
Entrepreneurs Association, Los Angeles, 1985.

Trade Journals

The Bowler's Journal
101 East Erie Street
Chicago, IL 60611
(312) 266–7171

The Bowling Proprietor
Bowling Proprietors'
Association of America
P.O. Box 5802
Arlington, TX 76011
(817) 460–2121

10

Building Material Retailers

Business Description (SIC. No. 5211)

Building material retailers primarily engage in the retail sale of brick and tile, cement, sand and gravel, lumber and millwork, roofing, siding, shingles, wallboard, insulation, and other building and construction supplies. This category also includes "home centers," which retail a variety of the aforementioned products.

Valuation Description

Building material dealers, even those favorably located, sell for minimal goodwill premiums. This is generally true of asset-intensive businesses, especially inventory-intensive ones. For the better stores, multipliers range between .05 and .08 of the latest 12 months of net sales. The value indicated by the use of the multiplier is for intangible assets only. Fixed assets should be restated at market value and added to the resulting value.

Net Equity Value

To estimate equity value, the value of net current assets, restated at market values less liabilities, is added to the value indicated by the use of the multiplier.

Valuation Considerations

Among the variables which should be considered in valuing a building material retailer are condition and market value of the inventory, location, competition, and lease terms.

Inventory

As in most asset-intensive businesses, the bulk of the value of a building material retailer is the value of the inventory. Building material retailers carry huge inventories, which must be revalued at the time of sale or on the valuation date. Obsolete items that are not likely to sell must be factored out. If the store is slow in turning over its inventory or has an inventory that shows obsolescence, a multiplier in the lower end of the range may be applicable.

Location

The location of a building material retailer is indicative of its success. It should have easy access, high visibility, and adequate parking. A prime location for a store catering to "do-it-yourselfers" tends to be close to, but not in, a shopping center, which draws potential customers. If the store caters primarily to professional contractors, visibility becomes less important; however, easy access for trucks is imperative. An industrial area might be best for this type of store.

The demographics and economic condition of the surrounding area should also be analyzed. The following questions should be asked.

1. What is the average household income in the surrounding area?
2. What is the typical profile of a home owner within the community?
3. What is the average cost of a new single-family home.?
4. What is the housing turnover rate in the area?

Areas with high housing turnover rates tend to spend more per capita on do-it-yourself home repairs than other areas.

Competition

It is critical to evaluate the competition within the five-to-seven-mile-radius market area of the subject store. Which buyers do the competitors cater to? What is the competitors' proximity to the subject store? Are they specialized? The greatest danger to the profitability of an independent building materials retailer is the presence or introduction of a chain mass merchandiser. The trend within the industry toward homecenter warehouses is forcing the independent retailer either to specialize or to offer extraordinary service. How would the subject store fare if a warehouse was introduced within the next six months?

The makeup of the customer base should be evaluated to determine the store's vulnerability to competition. If the building material retailer has a high percentage of business from contractors dealing in large volume, there may be a higher risk of consistent future revenues. Do-it-yourselfers tend to be loyal customers of a neighborhood building material retailer with an established reputation, whereas professional contractors often are more concerned with price than service.

Lease Terms

In establishing an appropriate multiplier, the current lease terms should be evaluated. The following items are important to consider in regard to lease arrangements: amount of monthly rent, right to sublease, and lessee responsibility for utilities and other expenses. A long-term lease with an option to renew would add considerably to the value.

Example

Step 1: Review and make a comparative analysis of income and expense for the previous
three years.

Income and Expense Summary
for 12 months ending June 30

	19x6	19x7	19x8
Net Sales	$497,553	$562,134	$581,321
Cost of Sales	359,233	405,860	419,713
Gross Profit	138,320	156,274	161,608
Operating Expenses	123,368	135,030	139,980
Net Operating Profit*	$ 14,952	$ 21,244	$ 21,628

* Depreciation, excessive owner compensation, and interest added back.

Note: It is important to consider income and expense trends as well as the current year's
(19x8) data. To more accurately predict future economic trends, the valuator should review
the most recent five years of financial data.

Step 2: Adjust the balance sheet to reflect the market value of tangible assets.

Balance Sheet Summary
as of June 30

	19x6	19x7	19x8	Restated at Market Value on Value Date
Assets				
Current Assets:				
Cash	$ 10,008	$ 12,788	$ 11,921	$ 11,921
Receivables	31,490	35,578	36,792	33,849
Inventory	110,147	142,479	165,816	154,956
Total Current Assets	151,645	190,845	214,529	200,726
Fixed Assets:				
Trade Fixtures and Equipment (net)	10,474	8,911	6,750	28,166
Total Assets	162,119	199,756	221,279	228,892
Liabilities	32,969	31,350	28,230	28,230
Net Tangible Equity	$129,150	$168,406	$193,049	$200,662

Example 81

Step 3: Apply the formula.

Formula Valuation Using Net Sales Multiplier

Net Sales (Fiscal year end 6/30/x8)	$581,321
Annual Multiplier	× .08
Indicated Value of Intangible Assets	46,506
Plus Adjusted Market Value of Tangible Assets	
Current	200,726
Fixed	28,166
Total Gross Value	275,398
Less Liabilities	28,230
Net Equity Value	$247,168

Sources of Further Information

Associations

DIY Research Institute
400 Knightsbridge Parkway
Lincolnshire, IL 60069
(312) 634–4368

National Lumber and Building
Materials Dealers' Association
40 Ivy Street, S.E.
Washington, DC 20003
(202) 547–2230

National Building Material
Distributers' Association
1417 Lake Cook Road, Ste.130
Deerfield, IL 60015
(312) 945–7201

Western Building
Materials Dealers
P.O. Box 1699
Olympia, WA 98507
(206) 943–3054

Publications

Books and Pamphlets

Almanac of Business and Industrial Financial Ratios, Prentice-Hall,
Englewood Cliffs, N.J., 1986.
Annual Statement Studies, Robert Morris Associates, Philadelphia,
1986.

Trade Journals

Building Supply
Cahners Publishing Company
1350 East Touhy
Des Plaines, IL 60018
(312) 635–8800

Home Center News
Lebher-Friedman Inc
425 Park Avenue
New York, NY 10022
(212) 371–9400

Home Center Magazine
Vance Publishing Company
400 Knightsbridge
Lincolnshire, IL 60069
(312) 634–2600

11

Carwashes (Coin-operated and Full-service)

Business Description   (SIC No. 7542)

Carwashes are establishments primarily engage in washing cars (full-service) or in furnishing facilities for the self-serve washing of cars (coin-operated).

Valuation Formulas

Coin-operated Carwashes

The most common valuation formula for coin-operated carwashes is based on a multiple applied to the latest annual net revenue. The multiplier ranges from 2.5 to 3.5, with 3 being typical. The value indicated by the use of the multiplier includes intangible assets, such as goodwill, and trade equipment including the wash building but not real property.

Full-service Carwashes

Valuation multipliers for full-service carwashes generally range from 17 to 25 times the monthly gross–net sales with 20 being typical and 25 for superior carwashes. The *gross–net* is defined as the gross income from all nongasoline revenue sources plus the gross profit from

gasoline sales. The value resulting from the use of the monthly multiplier is specifically for trade equipment (including the wash building) and intangible assets, but exclusive of real property.

Net Equity Value

To estimate equity value, the value of net current assets, restated at
market values less liabilities, is added to the value indicated by the
use of the multiplier.

Valuation Considerations

Among the factors that should be considered in the valuation of carwashes are location, reputation, condition and age of equipment, and
current lease terms.

Location

In an analysis of the subject location, visibility as well as accessibility
and traffic volume must be examined. Highly concentrated commercial districts and apartment neighborhoods tend to have the highest
revenue potential. Other prime areas are near or in shopping centers,
downtown areas, or business centers outside the downtown area. The
site should be on a main traffic artery or at least on a heavily traveled
secondary route. Preferably, it should be on a two-way street near a
major intersection with easily accessible ingress and egress. Carwashes located in areas such as these would command multipliers in
the higher end of the range.

The competition in the area should also be examined. This
analysis should include a review of the services provided by the subject business as compared to those provided by the competition.

Reputation

Because of the total service orientation of a full-service carwash,
reputation is one of the most important factors affecting goodwill. A
full-service carwash in a less than optimal location may have a high
sales volume if it has a reputation of providing consistently good ser-

vice. However, this would not hold true for a coin-operated carwash, which depends primarily on visibility.

Equipment

A careful inspection should be made to ascertain the condition of the existing equipment and premises. The older and more obsolete the facility, the lower the multiplier. If a great deal of renovation and modernization is required immediately, this will lower the multiplier further. Also, brushless carwashes are becoming more popular and could have a higher volume than brush-equipped carwashes.

Lease Terms

In valuing a carwash, careful consideration should be given to the existing lease terms. A multiplier in the high end of the range would assume a relatively long-term lease, with a minimum of 15 years remaining.

Example—Self-serve Carwash

Step 1: Review and make a comparative analysis of income and expense for the previous three years.

Income and Expense Summary
for 12 months ending June 30

	19x6	19x7	19x8
Net Revenue	$ 33,176	$ 42,859	$ 49,498
Cost of Sales	1,371	2,170	2,998
Gross Profit	31,805	40,689	46,500
Operating Expenses	27,144	31,754	35,762
Net Operating Profit*	$ 4,661	$ 8,935	$ 10,738

* Depreciation, excessive owner compensation, and interest added back.

Note: It is important to consider income and expense trends as well as the current year's (19x8) data. To more accurately predict future economic trends, the valuator should review the most recent five years of financial data.

Step 2: Adjust the balance sheet to reflect the market value of tangible assets.

Balance Sheet Summary
as of June 30

	19x6	19x7	19x8	Restated at Market Value on Value Date
Assets				
Current Assets:				
Cash	$ 5,348	$ 8,490	$ 8,981	$ 8,981
Fixed Assets:				
Trade Fixtures, and Equipment (net)	14,595	15,860	15,530	17,500
Building and Improvements	56,646	54,551	60,281	65,990
Total Assets	76,589	78,901	84,792	92,471
Liabilities	45,990	41,155	50,001	50,001
Net Tangible Equity	$ 30,599	$ 37,746	$ 34,791	$ 42,470

Step 3: Apply the formula.

Formula Valuation Using Net Revenue Multiplier

Net Revenue (Fiscal year end 6/30/x8)	$ 49,498
Multiplier	× 3
Indicated Value for Intangible and Fixed Assets	148,494
Plus Adjusted Market Value of Current Assets	8,981
Total Gross Value	157,475
Less Liabilities	50,001
Net Equity Value	$107,474

Example–Full-service Carwash

Step 1: Review and make a comparative analysis of income and expense for the previous three years.

Income and Expense Summary
for 12 months ending June 30

	19x6	19x7	19x8
Net Sales			
Carwash	$189,342	$195,844	$217,698
Gasoline	668,112	692,902	738,140
Total Sales	857,454	888,746	955,838
Less:			
Cost of Gasoline Sales	574,576	582,991	622,216
Gross-Net Profit	282,878	305,755	333,622
Operating Expenses	140,554	146,991	162,952
Net Operating Profit	$142,324	$158,764	$170,670

Step 2: Adjust the balance sheet to reflect the market value of tangible assets.

Balance Sheet Summary
as of June 30

	19x6	19x7	19x8	Restated at Market Value on Value Date
Assets				
Current Assets:				
Cash	$ 45,748	$ 51,465	$ 64,681	$ 64,681
Inventory	1,243	1,575	1,350	1,350
Total Current Assets	46,991	53,040	66,031	66,031
Fixed Assets:				
Trade Fixtures, Leasehold Improvements, and Equipment (net)	252,933	242,910	236,600	246,600
Total Assets	299,924	295,950	302,631	312,631
Liabilities	195,897	213,125	190,071	190,071
Net Tangible Equity	$104,027	$ 82,825	$112,560	$122,560

Step 3: Apply the formula.

Formula Valuation Using Monthly Gross–Net Sales Multiplier

Gross–Net Sales	$333,622
divided by 12	÷ ____12
Monthly Gross-Net Sales	27,802
Monthly Multiplier	×____22
Indicated Value of Fixed Assets and Intangibles	611,644
Plus Adjusted Market Value of Current Assets	66,031
Total Gross Value	677,675
Less Liabilities	190,071
Net Equity Value	$487,604

Sources of Further Information

Associations

International Carwash Association/National Carwash Council
One East 22nd Street, Suite 400
Lombard, IL 60148
(312) 495–0100

Publications

Books and Pamphlets

> *Almanac of Business and Industrial Financial Ratios*, Prentice-Hall,
>   Englewood Cliffs, N.J., 1986.
> *Annual Statement Stud*ies, Robert Morris Associates, Philadelphia,
>   1986.
> Chidakel, Myer R., *Starting and Managing a Carwash,* Small
>   Business Administration, Washington, D.C., 1967.

Trade Magazines

American Clean Car Magazine
American Trade Magazines
500 North Deerborne
Chicago, IL 60610
(312) 337–7700

Professional Carwashing
National Trade Publications
8 Stanley Circle
Latham, NY 12110
(518) 783–1281

Auto Laundry News
370 Lexington
New York, NY 10017
(212) 532–9290

Self Service Car Wash News
1410 Ardmore
Grand Rapids, MI 79506
(616) 243–0822

12

Cocktail Lounges

Business Description   (SIC No. 5813)

Cocktail lounges primarily engage in the retail sale of alcoholic drinks such as beer, ale, wine, liquor for consumption on the premises. They include

- — bars
- — beer gardens
- — saloons
- — taprooms
- — taverns

Valuation Formula

Value multipliers for cocktail lounges generally range from 4 to 9 times the monthly net sales. The value indicated by the use of the multiplier is specifically for trade fixtures, equipment, goodwill, and often the liquor license.

In states such as California, which allows the transfer of a liquor license from one owner to another, it is the general custom to include the value of the license within the multiplier. In states permitting such transfer the multiplier range would typically be between 6 and 9.

However, in some instances there may be reason to value the liquor license separately from the multiplier and add it to the indicated multiplier value. This is common practice in states with laws restricting the transfer of liquor licenses. Obviously, this practice would lower the value of the multiplier. In such instances, the multiplier typically ranges between 4 and 6.

Net Equity Value

To estimate equity value, the value of net current assets, restated at market values less liabilities, is added to the value indicated by the use of the multiplier.

Valuation Considerations

Among the factors that should be considered in the valuation process are the restatement of assets at market value, location, and lease terms.

Restating the Assets and Liabilities

Assets and liabilities should be valued at market. A major adjustment in value may have to be made to the liquor license. Licenses are often controlled by state agencies, and depending on restrictions for transferability, a license may develop a significant market value. A thorough analysis of the licensing laws should be conducted, as they differ substantially from state to state. For information regarding state liquor licensing laws, historical trends, and license market values, contact the local office of the state alcohol control department.

Location

Location is an important consideration in valuing a cocktail lounge. The valuator should analyze the neighborhood to determine the extent to which the establishment matches the community environment. Proximity to theaters, restaurants, and other bars, all of which draw crowds to the area at night, could protect the business from rapidly changing markets. Cocktail lounges located in metropolitan areas where trends and markets are changing constantly may be extremely risky ventures. Pending redevelopment in older areas may jeopardize the business if its function is not the highest income-producing use of the property.

Lease Terms

In establishing an appropriate multiplier, the valuator must also give careful consideration to the existing lease terms. A long-term lease with an option to renew would add considerably to the value of a cocktail lounge. In some instances the seller may also be the owner of the property, and a new lease must be negotiated.

Example

Step 1: Review and make a comparative analysis of income and expense for the previous three years.

Income and Expense Summary
for 12 months ending June 30

	19x6	19x7	19x8
Net Sales	$175,338	$192,844	$197,007
Cost of Sales	131,247	137,288	137,285
Gross Profit	44,091	55,556	59,722
Operating Expenses	31,554	31,626	32,489
Net Operating Profit*	$ 12,537	$ 23,930	$ 27,233

* Depreciation, excessive owner compensation, and interest added back.

Note: It is important to consider income and expense trends as well as the current year's (19x8) data. To more accurately predict future economic trends, the valuator should review the most recent five years of financial data.

Step 2: Adjust the balance sheet to reflect the market value of tangible assets.

Balance Sheet Summary
as of June 30

	19x6	19x7	19x8	Restated at Market Value on Value Date
Assets				
Current Assets:				
Cash	$ 8,932	$10,062	$10,651	$10,651
Inventory	1,293	1,575	1,350	1,350
Total Current Assets	10,225	11,637	12,001	12,001
Fixed Assets:				
Trade Fixtures,				
Leasehold Improvements,				
and Equipment (net)	13,824	12,642	14,464	26,715
Liquor License	9,251	9,251	9,251	30,000
Total Assets	33,300	33,530	35,716	68,716
Liabilities	2,438	2,125	2,071	2,071
Net Tangible Equity	$30,862	$31,405	$33,645	$66,645

Example 95

Step 3: Apply the formulas.

Formula Valuation Using Monthly Net Sales Multiplier Including Liquor License

Net Sales (Fiscal year end 6/30/x8)	$197,007
divided by 12	÷ 12
Average Monthly Net Sales	16,417
Monthly Multiplier (liquor license included)	× 7
Indicated Value of Fixed Assets, Intangibles, and Liquor License	114,919
Plus Adjusted Market Value of Current Assets	12,001
Total Gross Value	126,920
Less Liabilities	2,071
Net Equity Value	$124,849

Formula Valuation Using Monthly Net Sales Multiplier Exclusive of Liquor License

Net Sales (Fiscal year end 6/30/x8)	$197,007
divided by 12	÷ 12
Average Monthly Net Sales	16,417
Monthly Multiplier (liquor license not included)	× 5
Indicated Value of Fixed Assets and Intangibles	82,085
Plus Adjusted Market Value of Assets	
Current Assets	12,001
Liquor License	30,000
Total Gross Value	124,086
Less Liabilities	2,071
Net Equity Value	$122,015

Sources of Further Information

Associations

Distilled Spirits Council
of the United States
1250 I Street, N.W.
Washington, DC 20004
(202) 628–3544

National Alcoholic Beverage
Control Association
4216 King Street, W
Alexandria, VA 22302
(703) 578–4200

National Licensed
Beverage Association
309 No. Washington Street
Alexandria, VA 22314
(703) 683–6633

National Beverage Dispensing
Equipment Association
2011 I Street, N.W.
Washington, DC 20006
(202) 775–4885

Publications

Books and Pamphlets

> *Annual Statement Studies,* Robert Morris Associates, Philadelphia, 1986.
> *Almanac of Business and Industrial Financial Ratios,* Prentice-Hall, Englewood Cliffs, N.J., 1986.
> *Bars and Cocktail Lounges,* Bank of America Small Business Reporter, San Francisco, 1981.
> *Industry Norms and Key Business Ratios, Cost of Doing Business – Proprietorships and Partnerships,* Dun & Bradstreet, New York, 1986.

Trade Journals

Beverage Bulletin
8383 Wilshire Boulevard, Suite 252
Beverly Hills, CA 90211
(213) 653–4445

Beverage Media
161 6th Avenue
New York, NY 10013
(212) 620–0100

Beverage Retailer Weekly
250 West 57th Street
New York, NY 10107
(212) 582–1370

Licensed Beverage Journal
741 Boulevard East
Weehalken, NJ 07078
(201) 867–6380

Liquor Industry Market
Jobson Publishing Corporation
352 Park Avenue South
New York, NY 10010
(212) 685–4848

The Liquor Reporter
Smithwrite Communications
101 Milwaukee Boulevard
Pacific, WA 98047
(206) 833–9642

13

Coffee Shops

Business Description   (SIC No. 5812)

Coffee shops are moderate-service restaurants that offer table and/or counter service, employ food servers, and charge under $7.00 per meal. Such establishments do not serve liquor.

Valuation Formula

Valuation formulas for coffee shops are based on a multiple of the average monthly net sales. The multiplier generally ranges from 3 to 6, with 4 to 5 being typical. The value indicated by the use of the multiplier includes leasehold improvements, furnishings, fixtures, trade equipment, and intangible assets such as goodwill.

Net Equity Value

To estimate equity value, the value of net current assets, restated at market values less liabilities, is added to the value indicated by the use of the multiplier.

Valuation Considerations

Among the factors that must be considered when selecting a multiplier are location, competition, trade fixtures and equipment, historical income data, and lease terms.

Location

A proper location is possibly the single most important factor in a restaurant's success. Coffee shops tend to be the most profitable in densely populated business districts and along suburban traffic arteries. Heavy customer traffic that can generate large sales volume is considered essential to the survival of a coffee shop. Factors that should be noted when assessing population density are the number of households in the area, the activities (employment, shopping, or recreation) that draw people there, and the growth plans or potential for growth of the community.

The accessibility of the coffee shop should also be analyzed. A highly visible location at a traffic intersection can be beneficial, but the speed limit and the position of traffic lights, medians, and lanes should be noted to ensure that motorists may turn out of the flow of traffic to get to the site. Ample parking space and proximate public transportation facilities are desirable.

Competition

Competition in the area may also be a determining factor for the success of a coffee shop. Generally, restaurants compete only with the same food-service class. However, a local trend toward fast food franchises could entail a serious risk of loss of future revenues by the subject business. An analysis of existing and planned competition should be conducted to assess such risks.

Trade Fixtures and Equipment

The adequacy of the existing facility for both present and future needs must be assessed. Physical plant includes fixtures, trade equipment, and improvements. Factors to consider are

— the exterior image of the building

— signage which clearly and concisely states the restaurant's name and type
— the existence and condition of microwave ovens, waste compactors, food-holding areas and warming units, refrigerators, freezers, walk-in coolers, storage capacity, cleaning and sanitation devices, and carts to transport food and dirty dishes
— the amount and condition of serving pieces, china, glasses, and flatware

Kitchen equipment is expensive and can represent a significant portion of the total outlay involved in opening a new coffee shop. It is important, therefore, to evaluate whether the existing equipment is adequate, and whether there is any evidence of obsolescence. A coffee shop with inadequate or obsolete equipment would receive a multiplier in the lower end of the range.

The cleanliness and orderliness of the facility and the degree to which it is logically designed to facilitate work flow are also important considerations. The valuator should assess the adequacy of the work space to accommodate food preparation, passage of food from cooks to servers and from servers to customers, clean-up, inventory storage, and cold storage. Adequate space should be available to accommodate waiting customers when no tables are available and to serve customers once they are seated. Other spatial considerations include the adequacy of the eating room, the cashier station, and the public rest rooms.

Historical Data

Historical financial data and trends for the subject coffee shop should be analyzed and compared to industry averages. Information regarding industry averages can be found by contacting the National Restaurant Association (see sources at the end of this chapter). The data to be analyzed should include

— specific operating costs and expenses expressed as a percentage of sales and as amounts per seat
— daily seat turnover, sales per seat and average check
— sales per employee and sales per dollar of payroll and fringe benefits
— employee turnover rate

A review of the above will assist in the assessment of financial health. A well-managed coffee shop with consistently high operating ratios would receive a multiplier in the high end of the range.

Lease Terms

When valuing a coffee shop, the valuator must give consideration to the existing lease terms. Four types of lease payments are commonly found within the industry.

1. A base minimum rent versus a percentage of net sales; the lessee pays whichever is greater. The typical percentage is between 5 percent and 10 percent of net sales.
2. A base minimum rent plus a percentage of net sales over a specified amount; there may be a sliding percentage arrangement where the percentage applied decreases as the net sales volume increases.
3. Flat base rental where the rental payment is constant every month; this is an unusual type of lease payment that sometimes applies in small shopping centers or in the case of a land lease.
4. Percentage rent; the lessee pays a percentage of net sales, regardless of the amount of net sales.

The lease payment terms should be evaluated in the context of the location and type of site, that is, shopping mall or free-standing building. A long-term lease with an option to renew would add considerably to the value of the coffee shop.

Example 103

Example

Step 1: Review and make a comparative analysis of income and expense for the previous
three years.

Income and Expense Summary
for 12 months ending June 30

	19x6	19x7	19x8
Net Sales	$275,338	$292,844	$317,007
Cost of Sales	112,888	120,066	150,433
Gross Profit	162,450	172,778	166,574
Operating Expenses	137,669	146,422	153,503
Net Operating Profit*	$ 24,781	$ 26,356	$ 13,071

* Depreciation, excessive owner compensation, and interest added back.

Note: It is important to consider income and expense trends as well as the current year's
(19x8) data. To more accurately predict future economic trends, the valuator should review
the most recent five years of financial data.

Step 2: Adjust the balance sheet to reflect the market value of tangible assets.

Balance Sheet Summary
as of June 30

	19x6	19x7	19x8	Restated at Market Value on Value Date
Assets				
Current Assets:				
Cash	$ 28,232	$ 30,002	$ 26,651	$ 26,651
Inventory	9,923	11,570	12,050	12,050
Total Current Assets	38,155	41,572	38,701	38,701
Fixed Assets:				
Furniture, Fixtures,				
Leasehold Improvements,				
and Equipment (net)	79,402	83,144	77,402	85,055
Total Assets	117,557	124,716	116,103	123,756
Liabilities	12,938	16,125	9,071	9,071
Net Tangible Equity	$104,619	$108,591	$107,032	$114,685

Step 3: Apply the formula.

Formula Valuation Using Monthly Net Sales Multiplier

Net Sales (Fiscal year end 6-30-x7)	$317,007
divided by 12	÷ 12
Average Monthly Net Sales	26,417
Monthly Multiplier	× 5
Indicated Value for Intangible and Fixed Assets	132,085
Plus Adjusted Market Value of Current Assets	38,701
Total Gross Value	170,786
Less Liabilities	9,071
Net Equity Value	$161,715

Sources of Further Information

Associations

National Restaurant Association
311 First Street, N.W.
Washington, DC 20001
(202) 638–6100

Reference Center

Alice Statler Restaurant Library
City College of San Francisco
Ocean and Phelan Avenues
San Francisco, CA 94112
(415) 239–3460

Publications

Articles

Fraser, Dick, "How Much is your Business Worth?" *Restaurant Business*, August 1, 1981, pp. 85, 86, 88.
La Flamme, Gerald T., "The Purchase of a Food Service Business – A Value Judgement," *California CPA Quarterly*, September, 1979. pp.17–22.

Books and Pamphlets

Almanac of Business and Industrial Financial Ratios, Prentice-Hall, Englewood Cliffs, N.J., 1986.
Annual Statement Studies, Robert Morris Associates, Philadelphia, 1986.
Green, Eric F. *Profitable Food and Beverage Management: Operations*, Hayden Books, New York, 1978.
Keiser R. J., and Elmer Kallio, *Controlling and Analyzing Costs in Food Service Operations,* John Wiley & Sons, New York, 1974
Restaurants, Bank of America Small Business Reporter, San Francisco, 1983.

Rushmore, Stephen, *Hotels, Motels, and Restaurants –Valuations and Market Studies*, American Institute of Real Estate Appraisers, Chicago, 1983.

Stefanelli, John, *The Sale and Purchase of Restaurants,* John Wiley & Sons, New York, 1985.

Trade Magazines

Cornell Hotel and Restaurant Administration Quarterly
School of Hotel Administration
327 Statler Hall
Cornell University
Ithaca, NY 14853
(607) 256–5093

Nation's Restaurant News
Lebher-Freidman
425 Park Avenue
New York, NY 10017
(212) 371–9400

Restaurant Business
633 Third Avenue
New York, NY 10017
(212) 986–4800

Restaurant Hospitality
1111 Chester Avenue
Cleveland, OH 44114
(216) 696–7000

14

Coin-operated Laundries

Business Description   (SIC No. 7215)

Coin-operated laundries primarily provide coin-operated or similar self-service laundry and dry cleaning equipment for use on the premises.

Valuation Formula

Valuation multipliers for coin-operated laundries (coin-ops) generally range from 12 to 20 times the monthly net sales volume, with 14 to 16 being typical. The value resulting from the use of this monthly multiplier includes leasehold improvements, machines, trade fixtures, and intangibles such as goodwill.

Net Equity Value

To estimate equity value, the value of net current assets, restated at market values less liabilities, is added to the value indicated by the use of the multiplier.

Valuation Considerations

Among the factors that must be considered in the valuation of coin-operated laundries are location, condition and age of equipment, supplemental services, and current lease terms.

Location

Most coin-operated laundries service a market area within a two-mile radius. In an analysis of the area and location, the following questions should be considered.

1. What is the general income level of the customer base within the service area? (Communities inhabited by families with low to moderate income levels tend to use coin-ops on a more regular basis.)
2. Is the neighborhood subject to urban renewal with future industrial, apartment, or condominium developments planned? (A trend in the area toward the development of single-family homes potentially places a high risk on future coin-op revenues.)
3. Is the business close to, but not within, a shopping center? Does it have adequate customer parking?
4. How many competitors are in the area and what is the quality of their operations?
5. Are there any local codes or state licences that must be considered?

A coin-op with favorable answers to the above questions would command a multiplier in the higher end of the range.

Equipment

An inspection should be made to ascertain the condition of the existing equipment and premises, including washers, dryers, floors, lighting, boilers, water softeners, plumbing, and wiring. Any equipment more than five years old may need costly maintenance or replacement. Support equipment, such as coin/bill changers, detergent vendors and other vending machines should also be examined. The monthly net sales multiplier assumes that all equipment is owned.

New equipment would indicate the use of a high multiplier; equipment in poor condition would command a multiplier in the lower end of the range.

Because utility costs are a major expense for most coin-ops, the energy efficiency of all existing equipment should be carefully analyzed. Energy-saving features such as reduced gas use, extra insulation, preheated intake air, recirculated exhaust air, electronic pilot controls, and cold water rinses can cut utility expenditures dramatically. As a rule of thumb, businesses paying 28 percent or less of gross revenue for utility expenses are considered energy efficient.

Supplemental Services

Supplemental services should be reviewed as sources of additional revenue. Many coin-ops offer full laundry service by the pound to individuals and/or neighboring businesses. Commercial contracts should also be examined to determine their revenue potential and probability for renewal.

Lease

In valuing a coin-operated laundry, careful consideration should be given to the existing lease terms. The following items are important to consider in regard to lease arrangements: amount of monthly rent, right to sublease, responsibility for maintenance of leasehold improvements, and lessee responsibility for utilities, repairs, and maintenance expense. A long-term lease with an option to renew would add considerably to the value of the business. If the coin-op is located within a shopping center, the lease should include a restrictive clause prohibiting the leasing of space within the center to a competitor.

Example

Step 1: Review and make a comparative analysis of income and expense for the previous three years.

Income and Expense Summary
for 12 months ending June 30

	19x6	19x7	19x8
Net Sales	$144,227	$151,844	$153,011
Operating Expenses	93,554	90,391	92,955
Net Operating Profit*	$ 50,673	$ 61,453	$ 60,056

* Depreciation, excessive owner compensation, and interest added back.

Note: It is important to consider income and expense trends as well as the current year's (19x8) data. To more accurately predict future economic trends, the valuator should review the most recent five years of financial data.

Step 2: Adjust the balance sheet to reflect the market value of tangible assets.

Balance Sheet Summary
as of June 30

	19x6	19x7	19x8	Restated at Market Value on Value Date
Assets				
Current Assets:				
Cash	$ 12,648	$ 13,435	$ 14,651	$ 14,651
Accounts Receivable	1,243	1,575	1,350	1,200
Total Current Assets	13,891	15,010	16,001	15,851
Fixed Assets:				
Trade Fixtures,				
Leasehold Improvements,				
and Equipment (net)	52,933	51,910	49,464	65,000
Total Assets	66,824	66,920	65,465	80,851
Liabilities	35,897	33,125	32,071	32,071
Net Tangible Equity	$ 30,927	$ 33,795	$ 33,394	$ 48,780

Example 111

Step 3: Apply the formula.

Formula Valuation Using Monthly Net Sales Multiplier

Net Sales Volume (Fiscal year end 6/30/x8)	$153,011
divided by 12	÷ 12
Average Monthly Net Sales	12,751
Monthly Multiplier	× 15
Indicated Value for Fixed Assets and Intangibles	191,265
Plus Adjusted Market Value of Current Assets	15,851
Total Gross Value	207,116
Less Liabilities	32,071
Net Equity Value	$175,045

Sources of Further Information

Associations

Coin Laundry Association
1315 Butterfield Road Suite 212
Downers Grove, IL 60515
(312) 963–5547

National Automatic Laundry
and Cleaning Council
7 South Dearborn Street
Chicago, IL 60603
(312) 263–3368

Publications

Books and Pamphlets

Almanac of Business and Industrial Financial Ratios, Prentice-Hall,
Englewood Cliffs, N.J., 1986.
Annual Statement Studies, Robert Morris Associates, Philadelphia,
1986.
Coin-Operated Laundries, Bank of America Small Business
Reporter, San Francisco, 1979.
Opportunities for Energy Conservation in Coin-Operated Laundries,
San Diego Gas and Electric Co., San Diego, (no date.)

Trade Magazines

American Coin-Op
500 North Dearborn Street
Chicago, IL 60610
(312) 337–7700

Coinmatic Age
5 Beekman Street Suite 401
New York, NY 10038
(212) 349–3754

Coin Launderer and Cleaner
4512 Lindenwood Lane
Northbrook, IL 60062
(312) 272–8490

The National Clothes Line
717 East Chelton
Philadelphia, PA 19144
(215) 843–9795

New Era Laundry and Cleaning Lines
22031 Bushard Street
Huntington Beach, CA 92646
(714) 692–1351

Western Cleaner & Launderer
5420 North Figueroa Street
Los Angeles, CA 90042
(213) 254–2320

15

Dental Practices

Practice Description   (SIC No. 8021)

Dental practices comprise licensed practitioners who hold the degree
of Doctor of Dental Science and are engaged in the practice of general
or specialized dentistry, including dental surgery.

Valuation Formulas

Fixed and Intangible Assets

The primary formula for the valuation of established dental practices
involves the selection of a net revenue multiplier, generally applied
to the latest 12 months of net revenue. If the latest 12 months cannot
be considered normal, an average of the most recent two to three years
may be used. Net revenue multipliers generally range from .75 to
1.25. The results from this formula indicate the value for the fixed
assets and intangibles, including goodwill.

Intangible Assets Only

An alternative procedure calls for a separate valuation of the intangible assets. The indicated value for intangible assets may be derived
by use of the same procedure as the total valuation described above,
however, multipliers for intangibles generally only range from 30

percent to 40 percent. The resulting value includes such intangible items as going-concern (the incremental value generated by the assembled practice compared with starting up anew), covenant not to compete, and patient records. The value of fixed assets must be added.

Fixed Assets

Fixed assets such as trade fixtures, equipment, and tenant improvements can be valued at current replacement cost less depreciation or by market comparisons. (See Chapter 2.) The resulting total value for fixed assets is then added to the value indicated by the intangible value multiplier.

Patient Records

In valuing dental practices, a value may be developed for active patient records. The most commonly used method is the cost to recreate the existing active patient files. The cost of establishing a new patient file generally ranges from $30.00 to $50.00 per record. *Active patients* are defined as those who have actual billing records within the last 24 months.

Net Equity Value

To estimate equity value, the value of net current assets restated at market values less liabilities, is added to the value indicated by the use of the multiplier.

Valuation Considerations

Among the special factors that must be considered in the valuation of a dental practice are the transferability of the practice, patient characteristics, demographics, and lease terms.

Transferability

Different types of practices require specific transferability considerations. As a general rule, specialty practices that depend on a referral network may have minimal transferable intangible value. These referrals are usually attached to a specific practitioner rather than to the practice. If the referrals cannot be transferred to a buyer, a multiplier in the lower end of the range should be selected.

Some specialties, such as orthodontics, often have contracts with patients. If a substantial percentage of the practice is represented by such contracts, the quality of the income stream is enhanced and this will have a positive influence on the multiplier.

Practices that include contract associates may also have transferability problems. Associates are usually free to leave the practice at anytime, taking loyal patients with them. It will be necessary to adjust the multiplier and/or value of patient records to compensate for this factor.

Practice transferability tends to be superior when the seller grants use of his or her name to the buyer for a defined period of time subsequent to the sale and signs a letter of introduction to active patients. Retention of patient records, key staff, and the office telephone number can also decrease patient attrition and increase transferability.

Patient Characteristics

Patient characteristics should be examined before selecting a multiplier. These characteristics include age distribution, income levels, dental needs, treatment expectations, and prevalence of patient insurance coverage. The amount of time necessary to meet existing client needs must also be considered. These factors will dictate whether the practice is a four- or five-day-a-week business, and what amount of client base expansion is possible.

Demographics

Location often dictates the makeup of the client base as well as the fee structure. Demographic variables, such as age distribution and average household income, of the surrounding community should be examined to predict future revenue potential and associated risk factors. Practices in high income areas receiving higher-than-average fees can be more attractive to potential buyers and often command high multipliers.

Lease Terms

In valuing any small business, consideration should be given to the existing lease terms. The following items are important to consider in regard to lease arrangements: amount of monthly rent, right to sublease, and lessee responsibility for utilities and other expenses. A long-term lease with an option to renew would add considerably to the value of a practice.

Example 117

Example

Step 1: Review and make a comparative analysis of income an expense for the previous
three years.

Income and Expense Summary
for 12 months ending June 30

	19x6	19x7	19x8
Net Revenue	$121,971	$155,220	$157,009
Operating Expenses	105,065	133,815	130,178
Net Operating Profit*	$ 16,906	$ 21,405	$ 26,831

* Depreciation, excessive owner compensation, and interest added back.

Note: It is important to consider income and expense trends as well as the current year's
(19x8) data. To more accurately predict future economic trends, the valuator should review
the most recent five years of financial data.

Step 2: Adjust the balance sheet to reflect the market value of tangible assets.

Balance Sheet Summary
as of June 30

	19x6	19x7	19x8	Restated at Market Value on Value Date
Assets				
Current Assets:				
Cash	$ 10,002	$ 12,722	$ 11,319	$ 11,319
Accounts Receivable	7,869	8,129	9,144	8,321
Total Current Assets	17,871	20,851	20,463	19,640
Fixed Assets:				
Trade Fixtures,				
Leasehold Improvements,				
and Equipment (net)	27,886	26,387	31,791	37,000
Total Assets	45,757	47,238	52,254	56,640
Liabilities	33,481	29,594	31,628	31,628
Net Tangible Equity	$ 12,276	$ 17,644	$ 20,626	$ 25,012

Step 3: Apply the formulas.

Formula Valuation of The Total Practice Using Annual Net Revenue Multiplier

Net Revenue (Fiscal year end 6/30/x8)	$157,009
Annual Multiplier	× 80%
Indicated Value of Fixed Assets and Intangibles	125,607
Plus Adjusted Market Value of Current Assets	19,640
Total Gross Value	145,247
Less Liabilities	31,628
Net Equity Value	$113,619

Formula Valuation of Intangible Value Using Net Revenue Multiplier

Net Revenue (Fiscal year ending 06/30/x8)	$157,009
Annual Multiplier	× 40%
Indicated Value of Intangible Assets	62,804
Plus Fixed Assets	37,000
Total Value of Intangibles and Fixed Assets	99,804
Plus Adjusted Market Value of Current Assets	19,640
Total Gross Value	119,444
Less Liabilities	31,628
Net Equity Value	$ 87,816

Formula Valuation Of Patient Records

Price Per Record	$ 35
Number of Active Patient Records	× 1565
Value of Patient Records	$ 54,775

Sources of Further Information

Association

American Dental Association
211 E. Chicago Avenue
Chicago, IL 60611
(312) 440–2500

Publications

Articles

Beck, Leif C., "Guidelines for Buying into a Practice," *Dental Management*, September 1981, pp. 35–42

Bentley, Marvin J., and Jay Lieberman, "Goodwill–What Is It Worth in the Market?," *Journal of the American Dental Association*, September 1980, pp. 459–462.

Brunka, Victor, "Partner, Associate or Employee?," *Dental Economics,* May 1977, pp. 68–75.

Cohen, Ray Jeffrey, "It Pays to Appraise Your Practice," *Dental Management*, April 1981, pp. 44–48.

Coleman, Jack Rue, Leslie E. Kelton, Mark M. Meyers, and Richard O. Roever, "Evaluating Goodwill," *Journal of Clinical Orthodontics,* December 1981, pp. 833–836.

Dewey, Lawrence C., "So You're Going to Buy a Practice," *Dental Economics,* June 1972, pp. 30–34.

Dunlap, J.E., "What Is Your Practice Worth?" *Dental Economics,* May 1977, pp. 68–75.

Kallio, Dick, "Gross Not Major Factor in Setting Practice Value," *Dental Economics*, December 1981, pp. 39–42.

Pierce, Grant R., "How Much Is Your Dental Practice Really Worth?" *NYS Dental Journal,* April 1979, pp. 166–169.

Thompson, Gary W., "What's That Practice Really Worth?" *Medical Economics*, September 27, 1982, pp. 88–100.

Books and Pamphlets

Almanac of Business and Industrial Financial Ratios, Prentice-Hall, Englewood Cliffs, N.J., 1986.

Annual Statement Studies, Robert Morris Associates, Philadelphia, 1986.

Professional Management-Establishing a Dental Practice, Bank of America, San Francisco, Spring 1974.

Valuation of a Dental Practice: A Brief Overview for Buyers and Sellers, American Dental Association, Chicago, (no date.)

Trade Journals

✓*Dental Economics*
Pennwell Publishing Company
P.O. Box 3408
Tulsa, OK 74010
(918) 835–3161

Dental Management
Harcourt, Brace, Jovanovich
7500 Old Oak Boulevard
Cleveland, OH 44130
(216) 243–8100

Journal of Clinical Orthodontics
1828 Pearl Street
Boulder, CO 80302
(303) 443–1720

Journal of the American Dental Association
211 East Chicago Street
Chicago, IL 60611
(312) 440–2500

✓*Medical Economics*
P.O. Box 55
Oradell, NJ 07649
(201) 262–3030

16

Drug Stores

Business Description (SIC No. 5912)

Drug stores primarily engage in the retail sale of prescription drugs and patent medicines; they may also carry a number of related lines such as cosmetics, toiletries, tobacco, and novelty merchandise.

Valuation Formulas

The industry recognizes four market-derived formulas useful in establishing the value of a drug store. These formulas are based on multiples of net operating profit, average daily sales, and annual net sales volume. The use of these formulas results in a total business value, exclusive of real property, current assets (such as inventory), and liabilities.

Annual Net Profit Formulas

Two annual net operating profit formulas are used in the valuation process. One formula results in a total business value, whereas the other gives a goodwill value only. The total business value, inclusive of both fixed assets and intangibles, can be calculated by applying a multiple ranging from 6 to 7 to the most recent year's net operating profit.

To obtain a value for goodwill separate from the market value of tangible assets, a multiple of 1.0 to 1.5 should be applied to the latest year's net operating profit.

Average Daily Sales Formula

To use the average daily sales formula, the drug store's annual revenue should be divided by the number of days open per year (that is, if the store is open six days a week, the revenue should be divided by 312). A multiple of 100 should then be applied to the average daily sales figure. The resulting value is for tangible and intangible assets.

Annual Net Sales Volume Formula

The annual net sales volume formula estimates the store's total business value to be one-third of the net sales volume from the most recent 12 month period. If the latest year's sales volume cannot be considered normal an average of the latest two to three years can be used. The value indicated by the use of the multiplier is for tangible and intangible assets.

Net Equity Value

In order to value the net business equity, current assets including cash, inventory, and accounts receivable should be restated at market value and added to the tangible and intangible assets value indicated by the use of the formulas. Liabilities to be assumed should then be deducted.

Valuation Considerations

Factors that should be considered when valuing a drug store include location, competition, prescription files, transferability, and lease terms.

Location

Studies have found that 65 percent of a pharmacy's sales can be directly attributed to its location. Variables such as traffic count, visibility, accessibility, and adequacy of parking can greatly affect the profitability of the establishment.

Regional and local economic conditions should also be evaluated for a thorough locational analysis. The socioeconomic class served can have a dramatic effect on the type of facility and services that are necessary as well as on the status of accounts receivable. A pharmacy serving a clientele from an exclusive residential district will require a more spacious and prestigious pharmacy, finer fixtures and equipment, broader assortment of merchandise, generous credit, delivery, and various special services. A pharmacy located in a somewhat depressed economic area may find it necessary to furnish credit over long periods to an unusually large proportion of patrons. This would create a strain on cash flow thereby reducing the value of the store. A drug store serving a growing population in an exclusive residential district would obviously command a higher sale price and therefore a multiplier in the higher end of the range.

Other important considerations include the number and type of physicians practicing within the pharmacy's market area and their affiliation's with publicly funded programs and Health Maintenance Organizations (HMOs). According to the *Lilly Digest*, pediatricians and internists tend to write the most prescriptions, potentially increasing pharmaceutical sales within their service area. However, if the neighboring physicians are members or considering membership in an HMO, there would be no benefit to the drug store unless the store were also a member of the program.

Competition

The competition in the surrounding area should be compared on the basis of quality of service and product. A highly competitive situation may create a need for additional funds to finance a high level of advertising and other promotional activity, the sale of numerous products at low margins, and maintenance of a larger sales force to provide prompt service and frequent delivery service. These factors could contribute to an unusually low profit margin or stifled cash flow, lowering the value of the subject store.

The most recent competitive threat to the independent drug retailer is the introduction of Health Maintenance Organizations.

HMOs contract out prescription sales to chain drug stores with tremendous buying power who can offer pharmaceutical products at discounted prices. If the subject pharmacy exists in this type of competitive environment, it is important that it be a member of a Preferred Provider Organization or an HMO. Membership in such organizations can greatly increase the competitiveness of the store, thereby increasing the stability and profitability of the business. Typically, membership in such a program transfers with the sale of the business.

Prescription Files

When valuing a drug store, it is important to assess the present value of the existing prescription files. The files may be valued separately from other business assets by determining the proportion of refills that are still current. The number of refills should be multiplied by the average net profit on such prescriptions. However, different states have varying limitations on the refill life of noncontrolled substances. These restrictions should be checked to ascertain the number of prescription refills that are still of value.

Transferability

A pharmacy depends on the services and availability of a licensed or registered pharmacist. Because personal contact and confidentiality are necessary between the pharmacist and customer, it is important to determine whether the pharmacist will stay on after the sale or transfer of the business. If the pharmacist intends to leave, he or she should sign a covenant not to compete.

Lease Terms

In valuing any small business, consideration should be given to the existing lease terms. The following items are important to consider in regard to lease arrangements: amount of monthly rent, right to sublease, and responsibility for utilities and other expenses. A long-term lease with an option to renew would add considerably to the value of a drug store.

Example 125

Example

Step 1: Review and make a comparative analysis of income and expense for the previous three years.

Income and Expense Summary
for 12 months ending June 30

	19x6	19x7	19x8
Net Sales	$632,012	$659,934	$726,829
Cost of Goods Sold	410,808	433,457	457,275
Gross Profit	221,204	226,477	269,554
Operating Expenses	183,283	194,281	225,880
Net Operating Profit*	$ 37,921	$ 42,196	$ 43,674

* Depreciation, excessive owner compensation, and interest added back.

Note: It is important to consider income and expense trends as well as the current year's (19x8) data. To more accurately predict future economic trends, the valuator should review the most recent five years of financial data.

Step 2: Adjust the balance sheet to reflect the market value of tangible assets.

Balance Sheet Summary
as of June 30

	19x6	19x7	19x8	Restated at Market Value on Value Date
Assets				
Current Assets:				
Cash	$ 22,383	$ 30,268	$ 33,253	$ 33,253
Accounts Receivable	29,673	30,263	31,846	30,550
Inventory	90,378	94,370	103,936	99,875
Total Current Assets	142,435	154,901	169,035	163,678
Fixed Assets:				
Trade Fixtures				
and Equipment	32,252	29,872	26,744	30,250
Total Assets	174,687	184,773	195,779	193,937
Liabilities	40,964	36,869	31,388	31,388
Net Tangible Equity	$133,723	$147,904	$164,391	$162,549

Step 3: Apply the formulas.

Formula Valuation Using Net Operating Profit for Total Business Value

Net Operating Profit (Fiscal year end 06/30/x8)	$ 43,674
Multiplier	×_____6
Indicated Value of Fixed Assets and Intangibles	262,044
Plus Adjusted Market Value of Current Assets	163,687
Total Gross Value	425,731
Less Liabilities	31,388
Net Equity Value	$394,343

Formula Valuation Using Net Operating Profit for Intangible Value

Net Operating Profit (Fiscal year end 06/30/x8)	$ 60,674
Multiplier	×_____1.5
Indicated Value of Intangibles	$ 91,011

Formula Valuation Using Average Daily Sales

Gross Sales (Fiscal year end 6/30/x8)	$726,829
divided by number of days open per year	÷____312
Average Daily Sales	2,330
Multiplier	×____100
Indicated Value of Fixed Assets and Intangibles	233,000
Plus Adjusted Market Value of Current Assets	163,687
Total Gross Value	396,687
Less Liabilities	31,388
Net Equity Value	$365,299

Formula Valuation Using Annual Net Sales Volume

Annual Net Sales Volume (Fiscal year end 6/30/x8)	$726,829
Multiplier	×_____.33
Indicated Value of Fixed and Intangible Assets	239,854
Plus Adjusted Market Value of Current Assets	163,687
Total Gross Value	403,541
Less Liabilities	31,388
Net Equity Value	$372,153

Sources of Further Information

Associations

Affiliated Drug Stores
15 East 26th Street
New York, NY 10010
(212) 889–1560

American Pharmaceutical
Association
2215 Constitution Avenue, N.W.
Washington, DC 20037
(202) 628–4410

National Association of
Chain Drug Stores
P.O. Box 1417-D49
Alexandria, VA 22313
(703) 549–3001

National Association of
Retail Druggists
205 Daingerfield Road
Alexandria, VA 22314
(703) 683–8200

Publications

Books and Pamphlets

Almanac of Business and Industrial Financial Ratios, Prentice-Hall,
Englewood Cliffs, N.J., 1986.
Annual Statement Studies, Robert Morris Associates, Philadelphia,
1986.
Lilly Digest —1987, Eli Lilly and Company, Indianapolis, 1987.

Trade Journals

American Druggist
555 W. 57th Street
New York, NY 10019
(212) 399–3094

American Pharmacy
American Pharmaceutical
Association
2215 Constitution Avenue, N.W.
Washington, DC 20037
(202) 628–4410

American Journal of Pharmacy
Philadelphia College of
Pharmacy and Science
43rd Street
Philadelphia, PA 19104
(215) 596–8880

Chain Drug Review
Racher Press, Inc.
220 Fifth Avenue
New York, NY 10001
(212) 213–6000

Drug Store News
425 Park Avenue
New York, NY 10022
(212) 371–9400

NARD Journal
National Association of
Retail Druggists
205 Daingerfield Road
Alexandria, VA 22314
(703) 683–8200

Pharmacy Practice
American Pharmaceutical
Association
2215 Constitution Avenue, N.W
Washington, *DC 20037*
(202) 628–4410

17

Dry Cleaners

Business Description (SIC No. 7216)

Dry cleaners primarily provide laundry and dry cleaning services in a plant on the premises.

Valuation Formulas

The dry cleaning industry recognizes two market-derived formulas useful in the valuation of dry cleaning establishments that have a plant on the premises. These formulas are based on average monthly net sales and net operating profit.

Average Monthly Net Sales Formula

The average monthly net sales formula uses the monthly net sales averaged over a specific period (usually the most recent 12 months). If the dry cleaner has a plant on the premises, the revenue amount is most commonly multiplied by a factor ranging between 9 and 15, with 12 being typical. If the dry cleaner is an agency without a plant, it would be valued at 3 to 4 times monthly net sales. The resulting value is specifically for fixed assets, such as trade equipment and leasehold improvements, and intangible assets, including goodwill. Multipliers in the high end of the range tend to be applied to dry cleaning establishments with excellent locations and reputations, who have history of stable revenue.

Net Operating Profit Formula

The net operating profit formula can be used in valuing both dry cleaning agencies that contract out their work and dry cleaners with a plant on the premises. The formula applies a multiplier to the most recent 12 months of net operating profit. Multipliers generally range from .75 to 1.5, with 1.0 being typical. This formula results in a total for intangible value only. Fixed assets should be restated at market value and added to the intangible value indicated by use of the formula.

Net Equity Value

To value the total equity of the business, current assets including cash, inventory, and accounts receivable, should be restated at market value and added to the value indicated by the use of the formulas. Liabilities should then be deducted.

Valuation Considerations

Variables to be considered when valuing a dry cleaning establishment are location, condition of the equipment and facilities, existing contracts, and lease terms.

Location

The location of a dry cleaning establishment is the most important variable in determining success. The most desirable locale for this type of business is in a middle- to upper-income residential area with a high density of apartments and condominiums. Such areas tend to have a high concentration of singles and young couples with dual incomes. These demographics generate the highest dry cleaning revenue and indicate stability and profit potential.

Secondary locations include well-located strip centers catering to basic daily needs. However, centers focusing on the purchase of material items-record shops, bookstores, and so forth generally prove to be poor locations for dry cleaning establishments.

When evaluating the economic base of the market area, the following questions should be answered.

1. What percentage of people are employed full time and what is the trend in employment?
2. What is the average family income?
3. What is the per-capita total annual sales for dry cleaning services in the area.
4. What are home values and what is the percentage of homeownership?

Favorable answers to the above questions should indicate a primary location with a sound economic base.

Traffic patterns, visibility, and accessibility should also be examined. Industry statistics indicate that 72 percent of all dry cleaning is dropped off in the early morning, typically by commuters on their way to work. Conversely, 78 percent of cleaning is picked up after 4 p.m. An establishment located on a street carrying commuter traffic, which has convenient parking and is easily accessible (perhaps with a drive-up window), is a candidate for high revenue potential. Such a facility would tend to receive a multiplier in the higher end of the range.

Equipment and Facilities

The adequacy of the existing facility and equipment for both present and future needs is integral to the value of the business. Cleaning equipment is expensive and can represent a significant portion of the total outlay to open a new plant. Therefore, if the subject dry cleaner has a plant on the premises, it is important to evaluate whether or not there is any evidence of obsolescence. Factors that should be considered for a thorough analysis include

— the exterior image of the building
— the condition and energy efficiency of the major equipment including, dry cleaning unit, power plant, all-purpose utility press, legger utility press, automatic pants topper, form finisher, spotting board, and clothes conveyor
— the adequacy of the pick-up and work area

The condition of the facility, adequacy of work space, and appearance of the building are also determinants of value. Violations of local or state health or environmental codes that could jeopardize the licensing of the plant should be noted. Evidence of obsolescence or violations would significantly decrease the business value. Finally, any liens or equipment leases should be examined carefully to estimate value and transferability.

Contracts

It is common for dry cleaning plants to have contracts with various retail and service businesses in the community. If such contracts represent a significant portion of revenues, they should be examined to assess the longevity and loyalty of the client. Will the contract transfer upon the sale of the business?

Lease Terms

In valuing any small business, consideration should be given to the existing lease terms. The following items are important to consider in regard to lease arrangements: amount of monthly rent, right to sublease, and responsibility for utilities and other expenses. A long-term lease with an option to renew would add considerably to the value of a dry cleaning business.

Example 133

Example

Step 1: Review and make a comparative analysis of income and expense for the previous three years.

Income and Expense Summary
for 12 months ending June 30

	19x6	19x7	19x8
Net Sales	$275,020	$294,587	$303,142
Operating Expenses	235,536	242,464	248,998
Net Operating Profit*	$ 39,484	$ 52,123	$ 54,144

* Depreciation, excessive owner compensation, and interest added back.

Note: It is important to consider income and expense trends as well as the current year's (19x8) data. To more accurately predict future economic trends, the valuator should review the most recent five years of financial data.

Step 2: Adjust the balance sheet to reflect the market value of tangible assets.

Balance Sheet Summary
as of June 30

	19x6	19x7	19x8	Restated At Market Value on Value Date
Assets				
Current Assets:				
Cash	$ 28,487	$ 32,585	$ 38,573	$ 38,573
Accounts Receivable	14,297	15,474	18,473	18,255
Inventory	10,186	11,738	13,475	11,500
Total Current Assets	52,970	59,797	70,521	68,328
Fixed Assets:				
Trade Fixtures,				
Leasehold Improvements,				
and Equipment	181,300	160,854	140,847	195,750
Total Assets	234,270	220,651	211,368	264,078
Liabilities	71,948	67,014	56,235	56,235
Net Tangible Equity	$162,322	$153,637	$155,133	$207,842

Step 3: Apply the formulas.

Formula Valuation Using Average Monthly Net Sales

Annual Net Sales (Fiscal year end 06/30/x8)	$303,142
divided by 12	÷ 12
Average Monthly Net Sales	25,262
Multiplier	× 12
Indicated Value of Fixed Assets and Intangibles	303,142
Plus Market Value of Current Assets	68,328
Total Gross Value	371,470
Liabilities	56,235
Net Equity Value	$315,235

Formula Valuation Using Net Operating Profit

Net Operating Profit (Fiscal year end 06/30/x8)	$ 54,144
Multiplier	× 1.5
Indicated Value of Intangible Assets	81,216
Plus Market Value of Tangible Assets	
Current	68,328
Fixed	195,750
Total Gross Value	345,294
Liabilities	56,235
Net Equity Value	$289,059

Sources of Further Information

Associations

International Dry Cleaners Congress
P.O. Box 8629
San Jose, CA 95155
(408) 286–2969

International Fabricare Institute
12251 Tech Road
Silver Spring, MD 20904
(301) 622–1900

National Automatic Laundry
and Cleaning Council
7 South Dearborn Street
Chicago, IL 60603
(312) 263–3368

Textile Care Allied
Trades Association
543 Valley Road
Upper Montclair, NJ 07043
(201) 744–0090

Publications

Books and Pamphlets

Almanac of Business and Industrial Financial Ratios, Prentice-Hall, Englewood Cliffs, N.J., 1986.
Annual Statement Studies, Robert Morris Associates, Philadelphia, 1986.
Dry Cleaning Shop (AEA Business Manual No. X1037), American Entrepreneurs Association, Los Angeles, 1987.

Trade Magazines

American Dry Cleaner
American Trade Magazines
500 N. Dearborn Street
Chicago, IL 60610
(312) 337–7700

Dry Cleaners' News
Zackin Publications, Inc.
70 Edwin Avenue, Box 2180
Waterbury, CT 06722
(203) 755–0158

American Laundry Digest
American Trade Magazines
500 N. Dearborn Street
Chicago, IL 60610
(312) 337–7700

New Era Laundry
and Cleaning Lines
22031 Bushard Street
Huntington Beach, CA 92646
(714) 692–1351

The National Clothesline
Business Publications Services
717 East Chelton Avenue
Philadelphia, PA 19144
(215) 843–9795

Western Cleaner & Launderer
5420 North Figueroa Street
Los Angeles, CA 90042
(213) 254–2320

18

Fast Food Franchises

Business Description   (SIC No. 5812)

Franchised fast food restaurants primarily engage in the sale of hamburgers, hot dogs, donuts, ice cream, chicken, and ethnic foods (such as Mexican food). Many of these establishments also serve breakfast. Consumption may occur on the premises or on a take-out or drive-through basis.

Valuation Formulas

The industry recognizes two market-derived formulas useful in arriving at the total business value of a franchised food establishment. These formulas are based on multiples of the business's monthly net sales and net operating profit.

Monthly Net Sales Formula

Monthly net sales multipliers for fast food restaurants generally range from 4 to 12, with 5 to 9 being typical. The value indicated by the net multiplier includes fixtures, equipment, and goodwill.

137

Net Operating Profit Formula

Net operating profit multipliers range from 1 to 5, with 2 to 3 being typical. This formula results in a value for goodwill only. The fair market value of fixtures and equipment must be added.

Net Equity Value

In order to value the total equity of the business, current assets, including cash and inventory, should be restated at market value and added to the value indicated by the use of either of the formulas. Liabilities should then be deducted.

Valuation Considerations

Among the factors that should be considered in the valuation of a franchised fast food establishment are location, competition, franchise agreement, reputation, financial condition, fixtures and equipment, and lease terms.

Location

The quality of the location is possibly the most important factor contributing to the profitability and value of a fast food franchise. The site, as well as the surrounding area and region, should be examined. An analysis of the subject location should include an examination of visibility, accessibility, the volume of vehicular and foot traffic, and proximity to major thoroughfares and highways. Heavy customer flow and availability of adequate parking is considered essential to the survival of a fast food franchise. Fast food franchises are likely to be most profitable in densely populated business districts and along heavily traveled suburban traffic arteries. However, fast food franchises located in remote areas along state highways can also be very successful.

A general study of the surrounding area and a determination of the customer type (that is, nearby homeowner or freeway traveler) should be made. For example, freeway travelers and commuters are more prone to take out foods such as chicken, which has a longer holding time than other fast foods. On the other hand, hamburgers are mainly consumed on the restaurant premises. A hamburger franchise would tend to be more successful in a business district.

Regional food preferences that might exist among customers in different areas of the country should also be carefully researched. For instance, a roast beef sandwich chain might be very successful in the Midwest where large quantities of beef are consumed. In California, however, where the popularity of beef has dropped considerably, such an establishment might not be as financially successful (and, thus, less valuable). A careful evaluation of the current and future demand for the particular fast food type should be made. A volatile marketplace and changing consumer tastes add considerable risk. If the additional risk is substantial enough, the application of a multiplier at the lower end of the range might be warranted.

Competition

Competition in the area is a major determining factor of a fast food restaurant's success. An analysis of existing and potential competition, both franchised and independent, must be conducted in order to assess current and future risks. Generally, fast food franchises only compete with other fast food establishments that serve the same type of food.

Further, it is advisable to write to the franchise's regional or national office to gain insight into their future plans for expansion in the area and the franchise company's radius restrictions. Most franchise companies will not permit another unit to open in proximity to an existing unit if it is determined that the new unit will absorb more than 5 percent of the existing unit's revenue.

Franchise Agreement

The conditions and terms of the franchise agreement are important valuation considerations. An analysis of the agreement should include an examination of fees, degree of ongoing support, and extent and quality of the franchisor's advertising (marketing) efforts. Usually the franchisee must pay a monthly royalty fee and advertising contribution. The royalty fee generally ranges from 2 percent to 5 percent of gross sales. Advertising participation ranges from 1 percent to 3 percent for smaller chains and from 4 percent to 5 percent for larger operations. It is not unusual to pay a total of 8 percent to 9 percent of gross sales for popular franchises.

The franchisor's policy on renewing the franchise agreement should also be reviewed. Typically, franchise agreements for fast food restaurants extend for a period of 15 or 20 years. Such agreements are usually renewable for an additional 10 years, upon approval by the franchisor. However, by law, the length of the franchise agreement may not exceed that of the ground lease. If the owner of the real property is a third party, then the franchisor is limited in his ability to negotiate future renewals of the franchise agreement with the franchisee. Obviously, this situation is avoided if the franchisor owns the property.

Reputation

The fast food industry is both a product and service business. The reputation of such a business is primarily determined by the quality of its food and service. Reputation and public image are also influenced by the quality and amount of advertising done by the franchise company as well as the length of time that the franchise company and the particular outlet have been in operation. A high degree of public exposure and a solid reputation, built over an extended period, are important factors contributing to the amount of goodwill value possessed by a fast food franchise.

Financial Condition

A major valuation consideration is the degree of financial success that the franchise company has achieved. If the franchise company is publicly traded, the trends in the price of the stock and overall financial health of the company should be examined. A consistent decline in the price of stock, for example, might indicate that the reputation (that is, quality of food and/or service) is waning. Such a factor is important when considering the long-term success of the franchise.

Additionally, it is important to scrutinize the financial history of the individual franchise unit being valued. Historical financial data and trends for the subject should be compared to industry averages. The data to be analyzed should include: specific operating costs and expenses expressed as a percentage of sales and sales per employee and sales per dollar of payroll and fringe benefits. Generally, a fast food business must be established for at least 18 months before its operating results can be considered meaningful. A track record of three years or longer is preferable. In most cases, fads and other whims of the public (which might initially tend to inflate the sales volume) would level off over the course of three or more years. Such historical financial information is also helpful in indicating the influx of any competition in the area. A well-managed franchise, with consistently increasing sales and profit trends, would tend to receive a multiplier at the high end of the range.

Fixtures & Equipment

The adequacy of the existing facility for both present and future needs must be assessed. Kitchen equipment is expensive and can represent a significant portion of the total outlay involved in opening a new fast food restaurant. It is important, therefore, to evaluate whether the existing equipment is adequate and whether there is any evidence of obsolescence. A fast food franchise with inadequate or obsolete equipment may receive a multiplier in the lower end of the range.

Lease Terms

When valuing a fast food franchise, the valuator must give consideration to the existing lease terms. Four types of lease payments are commonly found within the industry.

1. A base minimum rent versus a percentage of net sales; the lessee pays whichever is greater. The typical percentage is between 5 percent and 12 percent of net sales.
2. A base minimum rent plus a percentage of net sales over a specified amount; there may be a sliding percentage arrangement where the percentage applied decreases as the net sales volume increases.
3. Flat base rental where the rental payment is constant every month; this is an unusual type of lease payment that sometimes applies in small shopping centers or in the case of a land lease.
4. Percentage rent; the lessee pays a percentage of net sales, regardless of the amount of net sales.

The lease payment terms should be evaluated in the context of the location and type of site, that is, shopping mall or free-standing building. A long-term lease (at least 10 years, preferably 20) and favorable payment terms would add considerably to the value of a fast food franchise.

Summary

The following grid rating will give the user some guidelines for a particular franchise being appraised.

	Low Volume and Cash Flow	Medium Volume and Cash Flow	High Volume and Cash Flow
Monthly Net Sales Multiplier	3–5	6–9	10–12
Annual Operating Profit	1	2–3	4
Volume	$100,000–$300,000	$3000,000–$700,000	over $700,000
Cash Flow (Percentage of net revenue)	0–5%	6–12%	over 12%
Accomodations	walk-up window only	some interior seating	interior and exterior seating and drive through
Location	marginal	good vehicular traffic	heavy vehicular traffic flow and/or expressway off-ramp
Lease	1–3 years remaining	5 or more years remaining	long term
Franchise Agreement	fair	good	excellent
Hours of Operation	limited evening hours	may be open until late evening	may be open 24 hours
Facilities & Fixtures	obsolete	some obsolescence	minimal obsolescence

Example

	Low Volume and Cash Flow		Medium Volume and Cash Flow		High Volume and Cash Flow	
Net Food Sales	$200,000	100.0%	$500,000	100.0%	$800,000	100.0%
Cost of Sales	68,000	34.0	157,500	31.5	232,000	29.0
Gross Profit	132,000	66.0	342,500	68.5	568,000	71.0
Variable Expense	78,000	39.0	185,000	37.0	272,000	34.0
Fixed Expense	48,000	24.0	110,000	22.0	168,000	21.0
Total Expense	126,000	63.0	295,000	59.0	440,000	55.0
Net Operating Profit*	$ 6,000	3.0	$ 47,500	9.5	$128,000	16.0

* Depreciation, excessive owner compensation, and interest added back.

Formula Valuation Using Monthly Net Sales Multiplier

Net Sales	$200,000	$500,000	$800,000
divided by 12	÷ 12	÷ 12	÷ 12
Average Monthly Gross Sales	16,667	41,667	66,667
Multiplier	× 4	× 8	× 12
Indicated Value of Fixed Assets and Intangibles	$ 66,668	$333,336	$800,000

Formula Valuation Using Net Operating Profit Multiplier

Net Operating Profit	$ 6,000	$ 47,000	$128,000
Multiplier	× 1.5	× 3.5	× 5.0
Indicated Value of Intangible Assets	9,000	164,500	640,000
Market Value of Fixed Assets	55,000	150,000	175,000
Total Indicated Value	$ 64,000	$314,500	$815,000

Note: For equity valuation using either formula, add adjusted market value of current assets, if any, less liabilities, if any.

Sources of Further Information

Associations

National Restaurant Association
311 First Street, N.W.
Washington, D.C. 20001
(202) 638–6100

International Franchise Association
1350 New York Avenue, N.W., Suite 900
Washington, D.C. 20005
(202) 628–8000

U.S. Small Business
Administration
1441 L Street, N.W.
Washington, D.C. 20416
(202) 653–6365

Consultants

Franchise America/Small
Business Center, Inc.
Benjamin Fox Pavilion, Suite A1
Jenkintown, PA 19046
(215) 887–7010

The Franklin Group
13212 Saticoy Street
North Hollywood, CA 91605

Publications

Books & Pamphlets

Annual Statement Studies, Robert Morris Associates, Philadelphia, 1986.
Directory of Membership 1986-1987, International Franchise Association, Washington, D.C., 1986.
The Franchise Handbook, Enterprise Magazines, Inc., Milwaukee, 1987.

Trade Magazine

Franchise Magazine
Franchise Magazine, Inc.
747 Third Avenue
New York, NY 10017
(212) 319–2200

19

Florist Shops

Business Description (SIC No. 5992)

Florist shops primarily engage in the retail sale of cut flowers, floral arrangements, and indoor plants.

Valuation Formula

The valuation formula for florist shops is based on a multiple of annual net sales. Multipliers commonly range from .40 to .50. The value resulting from the use of the multiplier is for fixed assets and intangibles.

Net Equity Value

In order to value the net business equity, current assets including cash, inventory, and accounts receivable, should be restated at market value and added to the value indicated by the use of the formula. Liabilities to be assumed should then be deducted.

Valuation Considerations

Factors that should be examined when valuing a florist shop are location, history and financial condition, affiliations, and lease terms.

Location

Because location can be the major determining factor in the profitability of a florist shop, it should be carefully scrutinized by the valuator. The following questions should be answered.

1. Is the site easily accessible and highly visible to pedestrians? (A corner location is considered optimal.)
2. Does the site have proximate, adequate parking?
3. Is the site attractive with adequate window space for displays?
4. How much competition, if any, is in the area?
5. Is the store located in a shopping mall where there is a great deal of foot traffic?
6. Are there nearby businesses that generate commercial accounts?
7. Is the surrounding community growing and viable?

A florist shop with favorable answers to the above questions would tend to receive a multiplier in the higher end of the range.

History and Financial Condition

The viability of the shop as a profitable business as well as its longevity and reputation must be assessed before choosing a multiplier. Specific operating costs and expenses expressed as a percentage of sales should be compared to industry data. The growth of commercial accounts as opposed to individual accounts should also be examined. Commercial accounts tend to be more stable as well as more profitable as business's consider flower arrangements a necessity, not an extravagance. When reviewing the records, the amount and age of accounts receivables should also be considered.

Affiliations

The multiplier that is applied to the net sales is ultimately a function of profit. If the subject business is a member of a wire service such as Florists' Transworld Delivery Association (FTD) or Teleflora, the wire orders received from these affiliations may represent a significant part of shop sales and, as such, a valuable part of the shop's profit. Membership with these wire services, therefore, is an important valuation consideration.

Note that membership in many of these wire services is not transferable to a new owner. Should a new owner be unable to qualify, the shop would no longer be a member and could not retain a portion of its clients and therefore its future profits.

Since the business profit pattern may change, so will the price a buyer will pay for the shop. If wire orders constitute a major portion of the business, it is imperative that a new owner be able to meet the application requirements of the services. If the shop was a member under a "grandfather-clause" listing, the listing granted the new owners may differ if they are not physically located in the city, town, or village where the shop is presently listed. For example, if a shop is located in a suburb of a major city that, when accepted by the wire service, was not incorporated, then the new owner will be listed for the suburb, not the major city. This could affect the volume of the new owner's incoming wire orders.

Lease Terms

In valuing any small business, consideration should be given to the existing lease terms. The following items are important to consider in regard to lease arrangements: amount of monthly rent, right to sublease, and responsibility for utilities and other expenses. A long-term lease with an option to renew would add considerably to the value of a florist.

Example

Step 1: Review and make a comparative analysis of income and expense for the previous three years.

Income and Expense Summary
for 12 months ending June 30

	19x6	19x7	19x8
Net Sales	132,557	139,185	146,144
Cost of Sales	62,302	65,417	68,687
Gross Profit	70,255	73,768	77,457
Operating Expenses	55,674	58,458	59,919
Net Operating Profit*	$ 14,581	$ 15,310	$ 17,538

* Depreciation, excessive owner compensation, and interest added back.

Note: It is important to consider income and expense trends as well as the current year's (19x8) data. To more accurately predict future economic trends, the valuator should review the most recent five years of financial data.

Step 2: Adjust the balance sheet to reflect the market value of tangible assets.

Balance Sheet Summary
as of June 30

	19x6	19x7	19x8	Restated at Market Value on Value Date
Assets				
Current Assets:				
Cash	$ 9,635	$ 12,472	$ 12,787	$ 12,787
Accounts Receivable	8,497	8,922	9,368	9,087
Inventory	8,306	9,345	9,812	8,831
Total Current Assets	26,438	30,739	31,967	30,705
Fixed Assets:				
Trade Fixtures, Leasehold Improvements, and Equipment	12,869	13,868	11,094	12,500
Total Assets	39,307	44,607	43,061	43,205
Liabilities	7,384	6,837	5,039	5,039
Net Tangible Equity	$ 31,923	$ 37,770	$ 38,022	$ 38,166

Example 151

Step 3: Apply the formula.

Formula Valuation Using Annual Net Sales

Net Sales (Fiscal year end 6/30/x8)	$146,144
Multiplier	× 45
Indicated Value of Fixed Assets and Intangibles	65,765
Plus Adjusted Market Value of Current Assets	30,705
Total Gross Value	96,470
Less Liabilities	5,039
Net Equity Value	$91,431

Sources of Further Information

Associations

Florist's Transworld
Delivery Association
29200 Northwestern Highway
Southfield, MI 48034
(313) 355–9300

Society of American Florists
1601 Duke Street
Alexandria, VA 22314-9990
(703) 836–8700

Publications

Books and Pamphlets

Almanac of Business and Industrial Financial Ratios, Prentice-Hall,
Englewood Cliffs, N.J., 1986.
Annual Statement Studies, Robert Morris Associates, Philadelphia,
1986.

Trade Journals

Florist Magazine
Florist Transworld Delivery
29200 Northwestern Highway
Southfield, MI 48034
(313) 355–9300

SAF Magazine
Society of American Florists
1601 Duke Street
Alexandria, VA 22314–9990
(703) 836–8700

Flowers&
Teleflora
12233 West Olympic Boulevard, Suite 140
Los Angeles, CA 90064
(213) 826–5253

20

Funeral Services and Mortuaries

Business Description   (SIC No. 7261)

Funeral services and mortuaries primarily engage in preparing the deceased for burial and conducting funerals.

Valuation Formulas

Within the funeral service industry, four market-derived multiplier formulas are used to estimate intangible value: net revenue, average gross profit, net profit, and the number of annual adult funerals.

Net Revenue Formula

The net revenue formula uses the average net revenue for a specific period, typically the most recent 12 months. The net revenue is usually multiplied by a factor between .70 and .80. The resulting number indicates the value for intangible assets only. The market value of fixed assets, (trade fixtures, equipment, and real property) must be added to the value indicated by the use of the multiplier.

Average Gross Profit Formula

The average gross profit formula uses the average annual gross profit for a specific period, usually one to three years. The average of these amounts indicates the value of intangible assets only. Fixed assets must then be restated at market value and added.

Net Operating Profit Formula

The net operating profit formula for estimating intangible value uses the adjusted net operating profit before income taxes for the most recent 12 months. If the last 12 months of net operating profit cannot be considered normal, an average of the last two to three years may be used. A multiplier of 3 to 5 is applied to the net operating profit figure. Again, fixed assets must be restated and added to the value indicated by the use of the multiplier.

Number of Annual Adult Funerals Formula

The number of complete adult funerals for the most recent year, multiplied by the average price for a standard service, is the basis for this formula. For example, if a funeral service operation conducted 75 adult funerals in its most recent year, and the average price of the funerals was $2,000, the intangible value for that funeral business is estimated to be $150,000. Fixed assets should be restated at market value and added to the value indicated by the multiplier.

Net Equity Value

To estimate equity value, the value of net current assets, restated at market values less liabilities, is added to the value indicated by the use of the multiplier.

In using these market formulas, it is not unusual to derive a broad range of intangible values. Experience has shown that the multiples of the net operating profit method and the number of adult funerals method tend to be in the lower end of the range of values, whereas the net revenue formula and the average gross profit formula tend to indicate a higher range of values.

Valuation Considerations

The major factors to be considered in valuing funeral services and mortuaries are restatement of assets and liabilities, ownership of real property, reputation, the type of facility and services offered, and demographics and location.

Restatement of Assets and Liabilities

The assets and liabilities must be restated at their market value near the date of valuation. Accounts receivable should be scheduled, aged, and analyzed according to their collectability, and a physical count of the inventory should be made near the close of the sale. Major assets such as real property should be appraised.

Real Property

It is common for funeral homes to own the property on which they operate. Given the rate of property appreciation in recent years and the high maintenance cost required for a mortuary, it is important for the buyer to analyze his occupancy cost at the location being purchased. Due to the major investment required to purchase the real property, it is not uncommon to relocate a mortuary to a less expensive area, still within the community, either prior to or after the sale of the business.

Reputation

Reputation, professionalism, and tradition are the basis of a funeral service's intangible value. The valuator should review the establishment's length of time in business in the community and the community's acceptance of its services. Community acceptance can be measured by increasing volume and increasing net income. Since the largest percentage of receipts is attributable to repeat family business, an establishment that has a long tradition of serving the community is far more valuable than a recently established mortuary. Because funeral service establishments depend on reputation, there is a significant intangible value for the business as a going concern, even if recently relocated.

Facilities and Services Offered

A thorough review of the condition and comfort of the facilities is vital in the valuation process. The construction of the funeral home should conform to the neighborhood. In addition, it should be well maintained and have adequate parking. The interior should have adequate chapels, embalming facilities, and a casket display area.

The services offered by the mortuary should be compared to services offered by competitors in the area. This is particularly true of pre-need services. An establishment that aggressively markets pre-need services not only increases its revenue and client base but also reduces business risk, particularly if the mortuary is located in a competitive environment. Mortuaries that offer pre-need services as well as extensive personal contact, personalized items, prayer cards, plates, and crucifixes tend to command somewhat higher multipliers than mortuaries with limited services.

Demographics and Location

Demographics, such as population density, age, ethnic distribution, and average household income of the surrounding community should be analyzed to predict future revenue potential and associated risk factors. Prime locations tend to be in family-oriented communities with a large population of senior citizens. The dominant ethnic groups in the area are also an important factor, as cultural practices often dictate funeral type and expense (that is, burial or cremation, with or without service). Any recent change in the makeup of the community should be carefully reviewed as it could potentially modify the revenue structure.

The accessibility of the funeral home is also important. The valuator should consider automobile and bus accessibility and convenience to churches and cemeteries. A mortuary located in a suburban area that is easily accessible and highly visible can be worth considerably more than a mortuary in a rapidly changing, crowded metropolitan area.

Example 157

Example

Step 1: Review and make a comparative analysis of income and expenses for the previous three years.

Income and Expense Summary
for 12 months ending June 30

	19x6	19x7	19x8
Net Revenue	$394,434	$418,670	$462,579
Cost of Merchandise	68,398	73,560	84,464
Gross Profit	326,036	345,110	378,115
Operating Expenses	260,713	279,570	309,334
Net Operating Profit*	$ 65,323	$ 65,540	$ 68,781

* Depreciation, excessive owner compensation, and interest added back.

Note: It is important to consider income and expense trends as well as the current year's (19x8) data. To more accurately predict future economic trends, the valuator should review the most recent five years of financial data.

Step 2: Adjust the balance sheet to reflect the market value of tangible assets.

Balance Sheet Summary
as of June 30

	19x6	19x7	19x8	Restated at Market Value on Value Date
Assets				
Current Assets:				
Cash	$ 24,847	$ 26,184	$ 28,146	$ 28,146
Inventory	36,865	37,940	39,310	35,000
Accounts receivable	7,187	9,730	8,211	5,859
Total Current Assets	68,899	73,854	75,667	69,005
Fixed Assets:				
Land	30,000	30,000	30,000	100,000
Furniture, Fixtures, and Equipment (net)	14,002	13,458	14,089	17,960
Buildings (net)	74,502	75,509	77,801	101,000
Total Fixed Assets	118,504	118,967	121,890	218,960
Total Assets	187,403	192,821	197,557	287,965
Liabilities	7,329	6,840	11,578	11,578
Net Tangible Equity	$180,074	$185,981	$185,979	$276,387

Step 3: Apply the formulas.

Formula Valuation Using Net Revenue Formula

Net Revenue (Fiscal year end 6/30/x8)	$ 462,579
Annual Multiplier	× .75
Indicated Value of Intangibles	346,934
Plus Adjusted Market Value of Tangible Assets	
Current	69,005
Fixed	218,960
Total Gross Value	634,899
Less Liabilities	11,578
Net Equity Value	$623,321

Formula Valuation Using Average Gross Profit Formula

Gross Profit:	
Year end 6/30/x8	$ 378,115
Year end 6/30/x7	345,110
Year end 6/30/x6	326,036
	$1,049,261
Number of Years	÷ 3
Indicated Value of Intangibles	349,754
Plus Adjusted Market Value of Tangible Assets	
Current	69,005
Fixed	218,960
Total Gross Value	637,719
Less Liabilities	11,578
Net Equity Value	$ 626,141

Formula Valuation Using Multiple of Net Operating Profit Formula

Adjusted Net Operating Profit (Fiscal year end 6/30/x8)	$ 68,781
Annual Multiplier	× 5
Indicated Value of Intangibles	343,905
Plus Adjusted Market Value of Tangible Assets	
Current	69,005
Fixed	218,960
Total Gross Value	631,870
Less Liabilities	11,578
Net Equity Value	$620,292

Example 159

Formula Valuation Using Number of Annual Adult Funerals Method

Complete Adult Funerals	
Fiscal year end 6/30/x8	187
Fiscal year end 6/30/x7	172
Fiscal year end 6/30/x6	+160
	519
Number of Years	÷ 3
Average Number of Complete Adult Funerals	173
Average Adult Standard Service - 19x8	$ 2,000
Average Number of Complete Adult Funerals	× 173
Indicated Value of Intangibles	346,000
Plus Adjusted Market Value of Tangible Assets	
Current	69,005
Fixed	218,960
Total Gross Value	633,965
Less Liabilities	11,578
Net Equity Value	$622,387

Sources of Further Information

Associations

Associated Funeral
Directors Service
810 Stratford Avenue
Tampa, FL 33603
(813) 228–9105

National Foundation
of Funeral Service
1614 Central Street
Evanston, IL 60201
(312) 328–6545

Continental Association of
Funeral and Memorial Societies
2001 S Steet, N.W., Suite 630
Washington, DC 20009
(202) 462–8888

National Funeral
Directors Association
P.O. Box 27641
Milwaukee, WI 53227
(414) 541–2500

Publications

Articles

Ninker, Robert W., "Your Funeral Home's Worth–Do Your Job Now," The Director, May/June 1984, pp. 5, 12, 13, 47, 48.

Pine, Vanderlyn R., "Measurement Procedures for Estimating Goodwill," *American Funeral Director,* January 1971.

Pine, Vanderlyn R., "A Method For Estimating Goodwill," *American Funeral Director,* February 1971, pp. 28–33.

Books and Pamphlets

Almanac of Business and Industrial Financial Ratios, Prentice-Hall, Englewood Cliff, N.J., 1986.

Annual Statement Studies, Robert Morris Associates, Philadelphia, 1986.

Nichols, Charles H., and Howard C. Raether, *How to Evaluate Your Funeral Home*, National Foundation of Funeral Service, Evanston, Ill., 1976.

Trade Magazines

American Funeral Director
1501 Broadway
New York, NY 10036
(212) 398–9266

Canadian Funeral Director
174 Harwood Ave., Suite 206
Ajax, Ontario
Canada L 1S 2H7
(416) 427–6121

Casket & Sunnyside
274 Madison Avenue
New York, NY 10016

Funeral Service "Insider"
2315 Broadway, Room 300
New York, NY 10024
(212) 873–3760

NFDA Reports
11121 W. Oklahoma Avenue
Milwaukee, WI 53227
(414) 541–2500

Morticians of the Southwest
2514 National Drive
Garland, TX 75041
(214) 840–1060

Mortuary Management
1010 Venice Boulevard
Los Angeles, CA 90015
(213) 746–0691

Thanatos
Florida Funeral Directors
P.O. Box 6009
Tallahassee, FL 32301
(904) 224–1969

The Director
11121 W. Oklahoma Avenue
Milwaukee, WI 53227
(414) 541–2500

The Southern Funeral Director
P.O. Box 7368
Atlanta, GA 30357
(404) 881–9780

21

Gasoline Service Stations

Business Description   (SIC No. 5541)

Gasoline service stations primarily engage in selling gasoline, lubricating oils and tires, batteries and accessories. Additional services may include maintenance and repair work, a convenience store, and towing.

Valuation Formulas

The gasoline service station industry generally uses three formulas in the valuation of service stations: the gallonage multiplier formula, the total services formula, and the net operating profit formula.

Gallonage Multiplier Formula

The key criteria in this valuation method is the number of gallons of fuel pumped per month as it relates to the average gallonage markup. Gallonage multipliers for dealerships range from $.75 to $3.50 per gallon of gasoline pumped per month. As the gallonage and/or markup increases, the multiplier increases accordingly. If the station only pumps gas, the multiplier would range between $.75 to $2.50. If the gas station is also involved in other income producing activities, such as operating a convenience store or mechanical repair service, the multiplier could go as high as $2.50 to $3.50. The resulting value includes the dealer-owned equipment and goodwill of the facility.

163

Total Services Formula

A second method of valuation is used to evaluate dealerships with other income-producing activities. To use this formula, apply a multiple of between $.75 and $1.50 to the average number of gallons of gasoline pumped per month. The appropriateness of the multiplier is primarily dependent on the gallonage and average markup. As the gallonage and/or markup increases, the multiplier increases accordingly. The net operating profit from other income producing activities should then be added to the value derived from the gallonage multiplier formula.

If the service station has a backroom repair shop, it should be valued at one year's net operating profit. Net operating profit is typically 30 percent of net revenue. This amount is added to the value indicated by the gallonage multiplier.

If the facility offers a convenience market, its most recent year's net operating profit should be added to the combined value indicated by the gallonage multiplier and the repair shop profit. As a general rule of thumb, a convenience store's net operating profit ranges from 20 percent to 30 percent of the net revenue.

The presence of other income-producing services such as towing, single bay carwashes, and detailing that contribute to the profit of the primary product would tend to increase the multiplier used.

The value indicated by the total service formula is specifically for the intangible assets of the business. Dealer owned equipment must be restated at market value and added to the value indicated by the sum of the service revenues.

Net Operating Profit Formula

The net operating profit formula applies a multiplier ranging from 1.5 to 3.5 to the annual net operating profit from the latest 12 month period. As with the other formulas , the appropriateness of the multiplier is dependent on the relation between the gallonage pumped and the average markup. The use of the formula results in a value for dealer owned equipment and intangible assets.

Net Equity Value

To estimate equity value, the value of net current assets, restated at market values less liabilities, is added to the value indicated by the use of the multiplier.

Valuation Considerations

The valuation criteria are the average gallonage per month and the average markup per gallon for the latest 12-month period. Additional factors that must be considered in the valuation process are length of the primary lease, type of lessor, type of dealership, size, and location of the facilities.

Gallonage Markup

Self-serve stations normally need to pump approximately 150,000 gallons per month at a 3 to 4 cent markup per gallon to make a profit. If a facility has less gallonage, it may need a convenience store and/or tune-up franchise to supplement income. Stations with both full and self-service islands can make a profit with less than 100,000 gallons if at least 30 percent of the gallons pumped are with full service. However, less gallonage may be required for a profit if other services are provided. For example, a backroom repair shop generating $15,000 to $18,000 of revenue per month can make a station profitable even if it pumps less than 65,000 gallons per month. Economic conditions affecting price and markup must be taken into consideration at the time of valuation.

Lease

The length and ownership of the primary lease is one of the most important valuation factors. At a minimum, the primary lease should have three years remaining. If the gasoline station's primary lease is owned by the oil company, the risk of lease cancellation is reduced due to state and federal restrictions. This decreased risk factor would increase the value of the dealership. However, if the primary lease is owned by a third party, the valuator should consider the time remaining on the primary lease in selecting the value multiplier.

Type of Dealership

The type of the dealership can affect saleability and value. It is important to consider the existing relationship between the station and the oil company and its field representative. Also consider the services and assistance they provide. Competitiveness of the cost of fuel and supplies and available rebates and incentives on increased volume should be reviewed. Credit card availability encourages repairs, especially high-priced services and tire, battery, and accessory purchases. Any service fee on credit cards imposed by the oil company is usually more than covered by gasoline discounts and the high profit of the service and repair facility.

Location and Layout

Further considerations in the valuation of a service station dealership are the location and layout of the facilities. The valuator should examine the surrounding community, as well as the traffic count and layout of the intersection or street involved. Accessibility is also important. Any barriers in the street, such as a concrete median preventing left turns, could make access to the station difficult and should be considered. The number of pumps and islands should also be evaluated for their adequacy in dealing with the volume of traffic. A station that always looks crowded due to an inadequate number of pumps or one that is not easily accessible could inhibit potential customers from stopping.

The term location does not just refer to the quality of the area. It also refers to the station's proximity to traffic patterns that will generate sales and the degree of competition in the immediate area. In particular, the station's proximity and visibility to a freeway or major highway should be evaluated. High visibility and convenient access to traffic patterns that can support the station are essential to its success.

Example 167

Example

Step 1: Review and make a comparative analysis of income and expense for the previous
three years.

Income and Expense Summary
For 12 months ending June 30

	19x6	19x7	19x8
Total Sales (from gallonage only)	$ 668,112	$ 692,902	$ 738,140
Cost of Goods Sold	574,576	582,991	615,429
Gross Profit on Gasoline	93,536	109,911	122,711
Operating Expenses	80,173	86,612	92,267
Net Profit on Gasoline	13,363	23,299	30,444
Other Income:			
Backroom Net Operating Profit	4,734	5,088	7,810
Convenience Store Net Operating Profit	3,330	4,291	5,911
Net Operating Profit*	$ 21,427	$ 32,678	$ 44,165
Annual Gallonage	723,819	743,581	721,824
Monthly Gallonage	60,318	61,965	60,152
Average Gallonage Markup	.11	.17	.17

* Depreciation, excessive owner compensation, and interest added back.

Note: It is important to consider income and expense trends as well as the current year's
(19x8) data. To more accurately predict future economic trends, the valuator should review
the most recent five years of financial data.

Step 2: Adjust the balance sheet to reflect the market value of tangible assets.

Balance Sheet Summary
as of June 30

	19x6	19x7	19x8	Restated at Market Value on Value Date
Assets				
Current Assets:				
Cash	$ 12,099	$ 17,721	$ 18,096	$ 18,096
Accounts Receivable	4,331	6,213	5,630	5,630
Inventory	38,490	30,538	34,999	34,999
Total Current Assets	54,920	54,472	58,725	58,725
Dealer Owned Equipment (net)	28,201	25,552	38,702	44,330
Total Assets	83,121	80,024	97,427	103,055
Liabilities	23,351	20,867	28,730	28,730
Net Tangible Equity	$ 59,770	$ 59,157	$ 68,697	$ 74,325

Step 3: Apply the formula.

Formula Valuation Using the Gallonage Multiplier

Average Monthly Gallonage	60,152
Multiplier	×$ 2.50
Indicated Value of Fixed Assets and Intangibles	150,380
Plus Adjusted Market Value of Current Assets	58,725
Total Gross Value	209,105
Less Liabilities	28,730
Net Equity Value	$180,375

Formula Valuation Using The Total Services Formula

Average Monthly Gallonage	60,152
Multiplier	× $ 1.25
Indicated Value for Gasoline Volume	75,190
Plus Additional Service Net Operating Profit	
Backroom	7,810
Convenience Store	5,911
Indicated Intangible Value for All Services	88,911
Plus Adjusted Market Value of Tangible Assets	
Current	58,725
Fixed	44,330
Total Gross Value	191,966
Less Liabilities	28,730
Net Equity Value	$163,236

Formula Valuation Using Net Operating Profit Formula

Net Operating Profit (Fiscal year end 6/30/x8)	$ 44,165
Mulitplier	× 3
Indicated Value of Fixed Assets and Intangibles	132,495
Plus Adjusted Market Value of Current Assets	58,725
Total Gross Value	191,220
Less Liabilities	28,730
Net Equity Value	$162,490

Sources of Further Information

Associations

American Gas Association
1515 Wilson Boulevard
Arlington, VA 22209
(703) 841–8400

Gasoline and Automotive
Service Dealers Association
6338 Avenue N
Brooklyn, NY 11234
(212) 241–1111

Gasoline Dealers of
America National Association
304 Pennsylvania Avenue, S.E
Washington, DC 20003
(202) 546–6868

New York State Association
of Service Stations
Eight Elk Street
Albany, NY 12207
(518) 434–6102

Publications

Books and Pamphlets

Almanac of Business and Industrial Financial Ratios, Prentice-Hall,
Englewood Cliffs, N.J., 1986.
Annual Statement Studies, Robert Morris Associates, Philadelphia,
1986.

Trade Journals

National Petroleum News
Hunter Publishing Company
950 Lee Street
Des Plaines, IL 60016
(312) 296–0770

Service Station News
New York State Association
of Service Stations
Eight Elk Street
Albany, NY 12207
(518) 434–6102

Service Station Management
Hunter Publishing Company
950 Lee Street
Des Plaines, IL 60016
(312) 296–0770

Super Service Station
Irving Cloud Publishing Co.
7300 North Cicero Avenue
Lincolnwood
Chicago, IL 60646–1696
(312) 588–7300

The American Dealer
Gasoline Dealers of
America National Association
304 Pennsylvania Avenue, S.E.
Washington, DC 20003
(202) 546–6868

22

Grocery Stores

Business Description   (SIC No. 5411)

Grocery stores primarily engage in the retail sale of all sorts of canned foods and dry goods, either packaged or in bulk (such as tea, coffee, spices, sugar, and flour); fresh fruits and vegetables; and frequently fresh, smoked, and prepared meats, fish, and poultry.

Valuation Formula

Value multipliers for small grocery stores generally range from 2 to 5 times monthly net sales, with 3 to 4 times being typical. This formula results in a value for the trade fixtures, equipment, and intangible assets, such as goodwill.

Net Equity Value

To estimate equity value, the value of net current assets, restated at market values less liabilities, is added to the value indicated by the use of the multiplier.

Valuation Considerations

Among the factors that must be considered when selecting a multiplier are location, presence of a license to sell liquor and/or beer and wine, condition of the facility and equipment, and lease terms.

Location

Location is probably the most important variable in the success of a grocery store. Most small grocery stores service a market area within a one-mile radius of the location. In an analysis of the area and location, the following questions should be considered.

1. What are the current and projected population figures in the area? (Generally, 750 people within a one-mile radius of the store site comprise an adequate market, assuming there is no other direct competition in the area.)
2. Are there schools, apartment buildings, commercial establishments, or parks that attract people to the area and would draw them past and, it is hoped, into the store?
3. Is the site on a major traffic artery as well as easily accessible and visible from the street?
4. Is the site on the side of the street that carries homeward bound traffic?
5. How safe is the area? (A grocery store in a high crime area would receive a multiplier in the low end of the range.)

Competition, both current and anticipated, must be evaluated. A supermarket in the area is not a direct competitor and can even boost sales. However, liquor stores and convenience food stores can seriously threaten the potential revenues of a grocery store. Pending redevelopment of an older area also might jeopardize the grocery if it is not the highest income-producing use of the property.

Beer and Wine License and Liquor License

An off-sale beer and wine license and/or liquor license can greatly enhance the goodwill of a grocery store and would indicate the use of a multiplier in the high end of the range. This is particularly true in competitive areas. However, if state law prohibits the sale of beer, wine, or liquor in food stores, the absence of the licenses should have a minimal effect on the value, as the competition is also prohibited from such sales. If the grocery has a liquor license saleable separately in the market, it should be restated at market value and added with the other current assets.

Equipment and Facilities

An inspection should be made to ascertain the condition of the existing equipment and facilities. Typical equipment includes frozen food cases, open-front beverage cases, wide island refrigerated cases, meat cases, and back room refrigerated storage boxes and shelves. Refrigeration equipment is expensive and can represent a significant portion of the total outlay to open a new grocery store. Because of this, it is important to evaluate whether there is any evidence of obsolescence. A grocery with inadequate or obsolete equipment would tend to receive a multiplier in the lower end of the range.

The cleanliness and orderliness of the facility and whether it is designed logically to facilitate speedy shopping is also a consideration. The back room should be examined to ascertain the adequacy and cleanliness of storage space for reserve stock, inventory, and produce preparation.

Lease Terms

In valuing a grocery store, consideration should be given to the existing lease terms. The following items are important to consider in regard to lease arrangements: amount of monthly rent, right to sublease, and lessee responsibility for utilities and other expenses. A long-term lease with an option to renew would add considerably to the value of the business.

Example

Step 1: Review and make a comparative analysis of income and expense for the previous three years.

Income and Expense Summary
for 12 months ending June 30

	19x6	19x7	19x8
Net Sales	$178,352	$185,844	$187,659
Cost of Sales	119,496	124,515	125,731
Gross Profit	58,856	61,329	61,928
Operating Expenses	44,588	46,461	46,915
Net Operating Profit*	$ 14,268	$ 14,868	$ 15,013

* Depreciation, excessive owner compensation, and interest added back.

Note: It is important to consider income and expense trends as well as the current year's (19x8) data. To more accurately predict future economic trends the valuator should review the most recent five years of financial data.

Step 2: Adjust the balance sheet to reflect market value of tangible assets.

Balance Sheet Summary
as of June 30

	19x6	19x7	19x8	Restated at Market Value on Value Date
Assets				
Current Assets:				
Cash	$ 12,258	$ 14,453	$ 11,521	$ 11,521
Accounts Receivable	549	621	657	592
Inventory	8,231	8,766	9,009	9,009
Total Current Assets	21,038	23,840	21,187	21,122
Fixed Assets:				
Trade Fixtures,				
Leasehold Improvements,				
and Equipment (net)	14,840	16,211	15,900	15,500
Total Assets	35,878	40,051	37,087	36,622
Liabilities	11,687	13,244	11,770	11,770
Net Tangible Equity	$ 24,191	$ 26,807	$ 25,317	$ 24,852

Example   175

Step 3: Apply the formula.

Formula Valuation Using Monthly Net Sales Multiplier

Net Sales (Fiscal year end 6/30/x8)	$187,659
divided by 12	÷ 12
Monthly Net Sales	15,638
Monthly Multiplier	× 4
Indicated Value of Fixed Assets and Intangibles	62,552
Plus Adjusted Market Value of Current Assets	21,122
Total Gross Value	83,674
Less Liabilities	11,770
Net Equity Value	$ 71,904

Sources of Further Information

Associations

Food Marketing Institute
1750 K Street, N.W.
Washington, DC 20006
(202) 452–8444

National Association of
Convenience Stores
1605 King Street
Alexandria, VA 22314-2794
(703) 684–3600

National American Wholesale
Grocers' Association
201 Park Washington Court
Falls Church, VA 22046
(703) 532–9400

National Grocers' Association
1825 Samuel Morse Drive
Reston, VA 22090
(703) 437–5300

Publications

Books and Pamphlets

Almanac of Business and Industrial Financial Ratios, Prentice-Hall,
Englewood Cliffs, N.J., 1986.
Annual Statement Studies, Robert Morris Associates, Philadelphia,
1986.

Trade Journals

Chain Store Age
425 Park Avenue
New York, NY 10016
(212) 371–9400

Grocery Marketing
23801 Gratiot Avenue
East Detroit, Michigan 48021
(313) 779-4940

Industry Focus
National Grocers Association
1825 Samuel Morse Drive
Reston, VA 22090
(703) 437–5300

Modern Grocer
Grocers Publishing Company
15 Emerald Street
Hackensack, NJ 07601
(201) 488–1800

Progressive Grocer
The Butterich Company
Department F
708 Third Avenue
New York, NY 10017
(203) 325–3500

Supermarket Business
Sosland Publishing Company
25 West 43rd Street
New York, NY 10036
(212) 354–5169

Supermarket News
7 East 12th Street
New York, NY 10003
(212) 741–4440

23

Health Clubs

Business Description   (SIC N0. 7299)

Health clubs provide exercise classes, fitness equipment and other fitness-related activities, including various indoor and outdoor sports, on a membership basis.

Valuation Formulas

The two formulas commonly used to estimate the value of health clubs are based on annual net revenue and net operating profit.

Annual Net Revenue Formula

The annual net revenue formula is based on a multiple of annual net revenue from the most recent 12-month period. Multipliers typically range from 1.5 to 2.0. The value indicated by the use of the formula is for tangible assets, including real property, and intangible value. The applicability of the multiplier primarily depends on available cash flow and the value of the real property.

Net Operating Profit Formula

The use of the net operating profit formula results in a value of the intangible assets of the club. Multipliers typically range from 1.0 to

1.5. Fixed assets, such as trade equipment, leasehold improvements, and real property must be restated at market value and added to the formula results. This formula would be most appropriate for a health club that leased rather than owned its premises.

Net Equity Value

In order to value the net business equity, current assets including cash, inventory, and accounts receivable should be restated at market value and added to the value indicated by the use of the formulas. Liabilities should then be deducted.

Valuation Considerations

Factors to be considered when choosing an appropriate multiplier include available market and location, membership trends, revenue ratios, condition of facilities, and lease terms (if the real property is not owned).

Available Market and Location

Because of constant membership attrition, the available market should be defined in order to assess future revenue potential. The geographic scope of the market area should be analyzed according to drive time and the nature of the facility. Acceptable drive time varies according to the density of the market and the availability of other alternatives. Typically, acceptable drive time varies from 8 to 10 minutes. The available fitness alternatives within that market area (typically a 3-mile radius) should be examined for market share and quality. This examination should include commercial clubs, country clubs, gyms, community parks, recreation facilities, and YMCAs or YWCAs.

The nature of the facilities and target market should also be analyzed. Because of time restrictions, a club aimed at the working population will generally have a narrower area to draw from than a club targeted for the residential population. Further, a multipurpose club will have a broader draw than a single-purpose facility.

The location of the site is also of primary importance to future profitability. An optimal site would be in the center of its primary market with high visibility and ease of accessibility. Proximate and adequate parking are also important.

Membership Trends

Four important operating ratios are crucial to gauging the financial success of a health club: membership growth, membership retention, usage per member, and club usage per day.

During the course of a year, every club will add new members and lose existing members, and at the end of the year the club will have a net figure either greater or less than at the beginning of the year. Within the industry, a net annual membership growth rate of 6 percent to 8 percent is considered good, 8 percent to 10 percent is excellent and 10 percent to 12 percent is outstanding.

The most important indicator of membership satisfaction and a prime indicator of long-term success is membership retention. Currently, the industry average is just under 30 percent. Clubs that keep attrition under 30 percent are considered to be very well managed; under 25 percent is considered outstanding performance.

Closely related to retention is club usage. Here, there are two important ratios, one for the club and one for the individual member. The object of knowing this number is to increase usage on the assumption that members who use the club more often will be less likely to discontinue their membership. A usage per day increase of 5 percent is good, 10 percent is excellent, and 15 percent is outstanding. More than 1.5 uses per member per week is good performance, more than 1.75 is excellent, and more than 2.0 is outstanding.

Revenue Ratios

Two significant revenue ratios should be examined when attempting to choose an appropriate multiplier: revenue per square foot and dues-to-ancillary revenue. These ratios are gauges of how well the club is faring in comparison with the industry as a whole.

Since consumer tastes change from year to year, revenue per square foot is a good indicator of how the consumer is responding to what the club is providing. As an industry average, for clubs without tennis (which because of the huge space involved skews revenue per square foot averages downward), $50 per square foot is considered good performance.

The second revenue ratio pertains to the sources of revenue. Most clubs today are dues-driven, with 70 percent of revenue coming from initiation fees and club dues. Ancillary revenue sources include guest fees, pro shop, restaurant, bar, locker rentals, tanning, hair salon, lessons, and classes. For every dollar collected in initiation fees and dues, the average club receives another 50 cents in ancillary revenue. One of the goals of the health club industry is to move the dues-to-ancillary revenue ratio from 70/30 to 65/35 to 60/40. A trend in this direction would indicate increased sales to current customers.

Facilities

The condition of the facilities and equipment should be assessed for a thorough valuation. As a result of the physical punishment clubs absorb, they deteriorate much faster than office or apartment buildings and require more repair and replacement. The club industry, being a retail business, is sensitive to change in consumer preference, and the club that does not recognize this by constantly upgrading and modifying its facilities would tend to receive a multiplier in the lower end of the range.

Lease Terms

In valuing any small business, consideration should be given to the existing lease terms. The following items are important to consider in regard to lease arrangements: amount of monthly rent, right to sublease, and responsibility for utilities and other expenses. A long-term lease with an option to renew would add considerably to the value of a health club.

Example 183

Example

Step 1: Review and make a comparative analysis of income and expense for the previous
three years.

Income and Expense Summary
for 12 months ending June 30

	19x6	19x7	19x8
Net Revenue	$589,475	612,874	$641,553
Operating Expenses	406,738	412,883	420,051
Net Operating Profit*	$182,737	$189,991	$221,502

* Depreciation, excessive owner compensation, and interest added back.

Note: It is important to consider income and expense trends as well as the current year's
(19x8) data. To more accurately predict future economic trends, the valuator should review
the most recent five years of financial data.

Step 2: Adjust the balance sheet to reflect the market value of tangible assets.

Balance Sheet Summary
as of June 30

	19x6	19x7	19x8	Adjusted to Market Value on Value Date
Assets				
Current Assets	$ 48,837	$ 49,763	$ 52,596	$ 52,596
Fixed Assets:				
Real Property & Equipment	610,839	590,754	560,962	828,170
Total Assets	569,676	640,517	613,558	880,766
Liabilities	319,764	300,537	292,639	292,639
Net Tangible Equity	$339,912	$339,980	$320,919	$588,127

Step 3: Apply the formulas.

Formula Valuation Using Annual Net Revenue

Annual Net Revenue (Fiscal year end 06/30/x8)	$ 641,553
Multiplier	×_____2
Indicated Value of Fixed Assets and Intangibles	1,229,106
Plus Adjusted Market Value of Current Assets	52,596
Total Gross Value	1,281,702
Less Liabilities	292,639
Net Equity Value	$ 989,063

Formula Valuation Using Net Operating Profit

Net Operating Profit (Fiscal year end 06/30/x8)	$ 221,502
Multiplier	×_____1.5
Indicated Value of Intangible Assets	332,253
Plus Adjusted Market Value of Assets	
Current	52,596
Fixed	828,170
Total Gross Value	1,213,019
Less Liabilities	292,639
Net Equity Value	$ 920,380

Sources of Further Information

Associations

International Racquet Sport Association (IRSA)
132 Brookline Avenue
Boston, MA 02215
(617) 236-1500

Publications

Articles

McCarthy, John, "Profitable Clubs & How they Do It: A Financial Model That Works," *Athletic Business,* March 1986, pp. 26, 28, 29, 30, 32, 34, 35.

Schwartz, Alan, "The Art and Science of Feasibility Studies," *Athletic Business,* April 1986, pp. 36, 38, 39.

Books and Pamphlets

Almanac of Business and Industrial Financial Ratios, Prentice-Hall, Englewood Cliff, N.J., 1986.

Annual Statement Studies, Robert Morris Associates, Philadelphia, 1986.

Caro, Richard, *Financial Management,* International Racquet Sports Association, Boston, 1986.

Profiles of Success - 1987 State of the Industry Report, International Racquet Sport Association, Boston, 1987.

Trade Journals

Athletic Business
Athletic Business Publishing
1842 Hoffman Street, Suite 201
Madison, WI 53704
(608) 249–0186

Club Industry
1415 Beacon Street
Brookline, MA 02146
(617) 277–3823

Club Business
IRSA
132 Brookline
Boston, MA 02215
(617) 236–1500

24

Insurance Agencies and Brokers

Business Description   (SIC No. 6411)

Insurance agents generally represent one or more insurance carriers. Brokers do not represent any particular carrier but act as independent contractors in the sale or placement of insurance contracts with carriers; they are not employees of the insurance carriers with whom they place contracts.

Valuation Formula

Valuation formulas for independent insurance agencies are based on a multiple of the most current 12 months of net renewal commissions. The multiplier generally ranges from 1 to 2, with 1.5 being typical. The use of the multiplier results in a value for normal amounts of fixed assets, such as trade fixtures and leasehold improvements, and intangible assets, such as goodwill.

Net Equity Value

To estimate equity value, the value of net current assets, restated at market values less liabilities, is added to the value indicated by the use of the multiplier.

Valuation Considerations

Among the factors that should be considered when selecting a multiplier are transferability, the present value of the portfolio of accounts, client and account characteristics, carrier characteristics, composition of the revenue stream, and lease terms.

Transferability

In the purchase of an insurance agency, it is general practice for the owner or key agent with the selling agency to stay with the new agency for a period of time. Failure of the seller to assist in the transition will, in all likelihood, increase the risk of client attrition and affect future revenues. Key employee-agents generally account for a high percentage of commissions, since they are most senior in the agency and have a higher percent of renewals. If the seller is not available, it is important to review the percent of commissions attributed to agents who will be retained and can help ease the transition period and increase client retention. A one-person agency may have limited transferable goodwill if the seller is unable to stay with the agency for an extended period of time subsequent to the sale of the business.

Portfolio of Accounts

In the valuation process, it is imperative to analyze the present value of the portfolio of accounts. Because life insurance accounts have a higher decay rate than property and casualty accounts, an agency specializing in life insurance may command a multiplier in the lower end of the range. This is particularly true in one-person operations where the main value of the business is in the portfolio of accounts. In a larger operation, other considerations beyond portfolio value (for example, qualification and reputation of the staff) may increase the multiplier and amplify the business value. If the agency handles both life insurance and property and casualty insurance the accounts should be analyzed separately to ascertain commission decay.

Client and Account Characteristics

The types of clients and their longevity with the agency are significant factors in developing a net commissions multiplier. The client files should be examined to determine the longevity of the association, age of the insured, what additional business has been written since the inception of the association, and the potential for increasing the policies. The industries represented by the agency and their vulnerability to economic cycles should also be considered. If the agency deals primarily in wholesale brokerage, the absence of client loyalty due to price sensitivity should be considered. Further, if the agency depends on one or two accounts for up to 35 percent of its business, the multiplier should be adjusted downward to account for the increased risk of attrition.

A higher multiplier is generally applied to agencies that have a healthy mix of business among personal lines, smaller commercial lines, and target commercial accounts. All three classes of accounts should be evaluated for vulnerability to competition and potential for retention. Are the lines well developed or are they single policy accounts? When were the accounts written? An agency with a healthy mix of accounts and a high account retention level would tend to receive a multiplier in the high end of the range.

Carrier Characteristics

A review of the carriers represented by the agency is important in ascertaining the stability and potential of the agency. Quality assessment factors relating to the carriers include: the claim count by carrier; size and stability; commitments required by the carrier; and longevity with the agency. What is the relationship between the carrier and the agency? Is the agency a member of a carrier Preferred Agent Program? Are there distinct differences among the carriers— some with casualty expertise, some with strength in property? Are these strengths being utilized by the agency?

Cash Flow

No two agencies have the same stream of cash flow and profit. One agency's business may consist of accounts that require few service expenses; another agency may contain many accounts that require a great deal of service. Obviously, two such agencies have different values. The net commissions formula does not take this fact into consideration, so cash flow should be considered when selecting an appropriate multiplier.

Lease Terms

In valuing any small business, consideration should be given to the existing lease terms. The following items are important to consider in regard to lease arrangements: amount of monthly rent, right to sublease and responsibility for utilities and other expenses. A long-term lease with an option to renew would add considerably to the value of an agency.

Example 191

Example

Step 1: Review and make a comparative analysis of income and expense for the previous three years.

Income and Expense Summary
for 12 months ending June 30

	19x6	19x7	19x8
Net Commissions	$429,492	$512,632	$589,938
Operating Expenses	394,703	471,108	542,143
Net Operating Profit*	$ 34,789	$ 41,524	$ 47,795

* Depreciation, excessive owner compensation, and interest added back.

Note: It is important to consider income and expense trends as well as the current year's (19x8) data. To more accurately predict future economic trends, the valuator should review the most recent five years of financial data.

Step 2: Adjust the balance sheet to reflect the market value of tangible assets.

Balance Sheet Summary
as of June 30

	19x6	19x7	19x8	Restated at Market Value on Value Date
Assets				
Current Assets:				
Cash	$ 59,758	$ 68,938	$ 91,116	$ 91,116
Accounts Receivable	153,903	160,197	184,355	75,228
Total Current Assets	213,661	229,135	275,471	266,344
Fixed Assets:				
Trade Fixtures and Leasehold Improvements	57,851	46,911	41,100	78,150
Total Assets	271,512	276,046	316,571	344,494
Liabilities	199,050	190,945	229,559	229,559
Net Tangible Equity	$ 72,462	$ 85,101	$ 87,012	$114,935

Step 3: Apply the formula.

Formula Valuation Using Annual Net Commissions Multiplier

Annual Net Commissions (Fiscal year end 6/30/x8)	$589,938
Annual Multiplier	× 1.5
Indicated Value of Fixed Assets and Intangibles	884,907
Plus Adjusted Market Value of Current Assets	266,344
Total Gross Value	1,151,251
Less Liabilities	229,559
Net Equity Value	$921,692

Sources of Further Information

Associations

National Association of
Casualty and Surety Agents
6931 Arlington Road, Suite 308
Chevy Chase, MD 20815
(301) 986–4166

National Association of
Health Underwriters
1000 Connecticut Avenue, N.W.,
Washington, DC 20036
(202) 223–5533

National Association of Independent
Life Brokerage Agencies
3299 K Street, 7th Floor
Washington, DC 20007
(202) 965–8998

National Association of
Insurance Brokers
1401 New York Avenue,
N.W. Suite 720
Washington, DC 20005
(202) 628–6700

National Association of
Life Underwriters
1922 F Street, N.W.
Washington, DC 20006
(202) 331–6001

Professional Insurance Agents
400 North Washington Street
Alexandria, VA 22314
(703) 836–9340

Publications

Books and Pamphlets

Almanac of Business and Industrial Financial Ratios, Prentice-Hall, Englewood Cliffs, N.J., 1986.
Annual Statement Studies, Robert Morris Associates, Philadelphia, 1986.
Neville, John F., ed., *A Guide to Perpetuation: Buying, Selling and Merging Insurance Agencies*, Insurance Marketing Services for the Independent Insurance Agents of America, New York, 1981.

Trade Journals

American Agent & Broker
408 Olive Street
St. Louis, MO 63105
(314) 421–5445

Best's Review
Ambest Road
Oldwick, NJ 08858
(201) 439–2200

Business Insurance
740 Rush Street
Chicago, IL 60611
(312) 649–5482

Insurance Review
110 William Street
New York, NY 10038
(212) 669–9200

The National Underwriter
1 Marineview Plaza
Hoboken, NJ 07030
(203) 963–2300

The Professional Agent
Professional Insurance Agents
400 North Washington Street
Alexandria, VA 22314
(703) 836–9340

25

Liquor Stores, Independent

Business Description (SIC. No. 5921)

Liquor stores primarily engage in the retail sale of packaged alcoholic beverages, such as ale, beer, wine, and whiskey, for consumption off the premises.

Valuation Formula

Valuation formulas for liquor stores generally are based on a multiple of monthly net sales averaged over a specific period (usually the most recent 12 months). Multipliers typically range from 3 to 6, with 4 to 5 being most common. The value indicated by the use of the formula is for fixed assets and intangibles.

In some states such as California, which allow the transfer of an off-premises liquor license from one owner to another, it is the general custom to include the market value of the off-premises liquor license within the value indicated by the use of the multiplier.

Net Equity Value

In order to value the net business equity, current assets including cash, inventory, and accounts receivable should be restated at market value and added to the value indicated by the use of the formula. Liabilities should then be deducted.

Valuation Considerations

Factors that should be considered when valuing a liquor store include location, state regulations on alcoholic beverages, method of operation, and lease terms.

Location

Location is the most important variable in the success of a liquor store. In an analysis of the area and location, the following questions should be considered.

1. What are the current and projected population figures for the area?
2. Is the site on a major traffic artery. Is it easily accessible and visible from the street?
3. Is the site on the side of the street that carries homeward bound traffic?
4. How safe is the area? (A store in a high crime area would tend to receive a multiplier in the low end or the range.)

Competition, both current and anticipated, must also be evaluated. Convenience food stores and small grocery stores can seriously threaten the potential profitability of a liquor store. Pending redevelopment of an older area also might jeopardize the store if is not the highest income-producing use of the property.

State Regulations

The applicability of the formula primarily depends on the existing state and local codes restricting the sale of alcoholic beverages and/or the transferability of a liquor license. If the liquor license is transferable to a new owner, it may develop a significant market value separate from the business. A thorough analysis of the licensing laws should be conducted as they differ substantially from state to state, For information regarding state liquor licensing laws, historical trends, and license market values, contact the local office of the state alcohol control department.

Method of Operation

Another factor in valuing a liquor store has to do with an owner/operator versus an absentee-run business. Two liquor stores, store A and store B, with a similar gross, net operating profit structure, and lease may have dissimilar values if A is run by employees and B is operated by the owner. If store A has strong management in place, this can be an asset to the potential new owner, who can choose to leave well enough alone or decide to come in and operate the business thereby raising the profit. Store B doesn't have this luxury. The new owner is simply "buying himself a job." When the owner/operator sells, the sales volume may drop due to the owner's relationship with his customers. Although owner/operator businesses can be outstanding investments, they must be studied carefully to ascertain what effect the owner's leaving will have on the business.

Lease Terms

In valuing any small business, consideration should be given to the existing lease terms. The following items are important to consider in regard to lease arrangements: amount of monthly rent, right to sublease, and responsibility for utilities and other expenses. A long-term lease with an option to renew would add considerably to the value of a liquor store.

Example

Step 1: Review and make a comparative analysis of income and expense for the previous three years.

Income and Expense Summary
for 12 months ending June 30

	19x6	19x7	19x8
Net Sales	$340,932	$364,797	$390,333
Cost of Sales	265,927	280,894	300,556
Gross Profit	75,005	83,903	89,777
Operating Expenses	61,367	65,663	70,260
Net Operating Profit*	$ 13,638	$ 18,240	$ 19,517

* Depreciation, excessive owner compensation, and interest added back.

Note: It is important to consider income and expense trends as well as the current year's (19x8) data. To more accurately predict future economic trends, the valuator should review the most recent five years of financial data.

Step 2: Adjust the balance sheet to reflect the market value of tangible assets.

Balance Sheet Summary
as of June 30

	19x6	19x7	19x8	Adjusted to Market Value on Value Date
Assets				
Current Assets:				
Cash	5,053	5,362	5,806	5,806
Inventory	30,219	31,920	34,154	33,109
Total Current Assets	35,272	37,282	39,960	38,915
Fixed Assets:				
Trade Fixtures,				
Leasehold Improvements,				
and Equipment	17,238	20,549	18,239	19,950
Total Assets	52,510	57,831	58,199	58,865
Liabilities	21,439	19,583	17,483	17,483
Net Tangible Equity	$ 31,071	$ 38,248	$ 40,716	$ 41,382

Example 199

Step 3: Apply the formula.

Formula Valuation Using Average Monthly Net Sales

Net Sales (Fiscal year end 06/30/x8)	$390,333
divided by 12	÷ 12
Average Monthly Gross Sales	35,528
Multiplier	× 5
Indicated Value of Fixed Assets and Intangibles	162,640
Plus Adjusted Market Value of Current Assets	38,915
Total Gross Value	201,555
Less Liabilities	17,483
Net Equity Value	$219,038

Sources of Further Information

Associations

National Alcoholic Beverage Control Association
4216 King Street, W.
Alexandria, VA 22302
(703) 578–4200

National Liquor Stores Association
5101 River Road, Suite 108
Bethesda, MD 20816
(301) 656–1494

Publications

Books and Pamphlets

> *Almanac of Business and Industrial Financial Ratios,* Prentice-Hall, Englewood Cliffs, N.J., 1986.
> *Annual Statement Studies*, Robert Morris Associates, Philadelphia, 1986.

Trade Journal

Liquor Store Magazine
Jobson Publishing Company
352 Park Avenue South, 16th Floor
New York, NY 10010
(212) 685–4848

26

Manufacturers' Sales Agencies

Business Description

Manufacturers' sales agencies act as agents or brokers in selling merchandise to retailers and to industrial, commercial, institutional, farm, and professional business users. In addition to selling, these agencies frequently offer services such as maintaining inventories of goods and various types of promotion such as advertising and label design.

Valuation Formulas

Two market-derived multiplier formulas are used in estimating the value of a manufacturers' sales agency. They are based on multiples of annual net commissions and net operating profit.

Net Commissions Formula

The net commissions formula is based on a multiple of the most current 12 months of net commission income, plus the net tangible asset value. The multiplier generally ranges from 1 to 1.5. Allowances for earned commissions for goods shipped but not yet received, as well as unearned commissions for signed orders where the goods have not been shipped, should be added to the value indicated by use of the multiplier.

Unearned commissions, although difficult to value, may represent a major unrecorded asset of the agency. It is important to ascertain whether the order is firm and virtually noncancellable. Even if the order is firm, the right to receive a $10,000 commission in the future is not worth $10,000 at the present time.

The value indicated by the use of the multiplier is specifically for intangible assets. To complete the valuation, fixed assets, such as trade fixtures and equipment, must be added to the value indicated by the use of the multiplier.

Net Operating Profit Formula

This procedure for estimating the value of an agency calls for multiplying the adjusted net operating profit (before owner's salary and income taxes) for the most recent 12 months by a multiple of 2 to 5. Fixed assets must then be restated at market value and added to the value indicated by the use of the multiplier.

Net Equity Value

To estimate equity value, the value of net current assets, restated at market values less liabilities, is added to the value indicated by the use of the multiplier.

Valuation Considerations

Among the factors that should be considered in the valuation of a manufacturers' sales agency are transferability, manufacturer and product characteristics, revenue mix, and lease terms.

Transferability

In the purchase of manufacturers' sales agencies, it is general practice for the owner or key employee/agent with the selling company to stay with the new agency for a period of time. Failure of the seller to assist in the transition will, in all likelihood, affect future revenues due to probable attrition of manufacturer accounts. If the seller is not available, it is important to review the percent of the revenues attributed to the staff who will be retained to help ease the transition period and increase manufacturer retention. This factor tends to be particularly significant when the buyer is not a seasoned member of the agency staff.

Manufacturer and Product Characteristics

Characteristics of the manufacturers and their longevity with the agency are significant variables in developing a multiplier. The quality assessment factors relating to manufacturers that should be reviewed include industry classification, geographic distribution, maturity of the company, number of lines carried, record of payment for commissions, other services rendered, growth potential, and relationship with the staff and principals of the agency.

The quality and marketability of the product lines should also be assessed. Is the market expanding or decreasing? How innovative is the manufacturer with regard to product development? An agency representing quality manufacturers with highly marketable product lines would tend to receive a multiplier in the higher end of the range.

Revenue Mix

The actual number of manufacturers represented and commission dispersion among them may be an indicator of potential ease of transferability. Most agencies have between one and three manufacturers that comprise over 50 percent of their business. The loss of one major manufacturer may reduce revenues by 20 percent to 60 percent. One suggested method of developing a net commissions multiplier is to apply a different multiplier to each manufacturer based on probable retention levels. A sample of this method is shown below.

Example of
Percentage of Net Commissions Method

	Manufacturer				
	1	2	3	Others	Total
Percent of Total Commissions	35%	20%	25%	20%	100%
Estimated net commissions multiplier	1.0	1.5	1.5	1.0	
Weighted percent	.35	.30	.375	.2	1.225
					rounded to 1.25

Lease Terms

In valuing any small business, consideration should be given to the existing lease terms. The following items are important to consider in regard to lease arrangements: amount of monthly rent, right to sub-lease and responsibility for utilities and other expenses. A long-term lease with an option to renew would add considerably to the value of a business.

Example 205

Example

Step 1: Review and make a comparative analysis of income and expense for the previous three years.

Income and Expense Summary
for 12 months ending June 30

	19x6	19x7	19x8
Net Commissions	$478,992	$545,432	$610,758
Owner's Salary	85,000	95,000	100,000
Other Operating Expenses	212,699	304,545	362,573
Net Operating Profit*	$181,293	$145,887	$148,185

* Depreciation, excessive owner compensation, and interest added back.

Note: It is important to consider income and expense trends as well as the current year's (19x8) data. To more accurately predict future economic trends, the valuator should review the most recent five years of financial data.

Step 2: Adjust the balance sheet to reflect the market value of tangible assets.

Balance Sheet Summary
as of June 30

	19x6	19x7	19x8	Restated at Market Value on Value Date
Assets				
Current Assets:				
Cash	$ 69,480	$ 73,295	$ 81,112	$ 81,112
Accounts Receivable	98,355	72,873	102,873	98,655
Total Current Assets	167,835	146,168	183,985	179,767
Fixed Assets:				
Trade Fixtures,				
Leasehold Improvements,				
and Equipment (net)	68,554	65,188	70,142	105,000
Total Assets	236,389	211,356	254,127	284,767
Liabilities	78,395	85,534	79,834	79,834
Net Tangible Equity	$157,994	$125,822	$174,293	$204,933

Step 3: Apply the formulas.

Formula Valuation Using Net Commissions Multiplier

Net Commissions (Fiscal year end 6/30/x8)	$ 610,758
Multiplier	× 1.25
Indicated Value of Intangible Assets	763,448
Plus:	
Earned Commissions	22,065
Unearned Commissions	10,000
Plus Adjusted Market Value of Tangible Assets	
Current	179,766
Fixed	105,000
Total Gross Value	1,080,279
Less Liabilities	79,834
Net Equity Value	$1,000,445

Formula Valuation Using Net Operating Profit Multiplier

Net Operating Profit (Fiscal year end 6/30/x8)	$ 148,185
Plus Owner's Salary	100,000
Adjusted Net Operating Profit	248,185
Annual Multiplier	× 3
Indicated Value of Intangible Assets	744,555
Plus Adjusted Market Value of Tangible Assets	
Current	179,767
Fixed	105,000
Total Gross Value	1,029,322
Less Liabilities	79,834
Net Equity Value	$ 949,488

Sources of Further Information

Associations

Manufacturers' Agents
National Association
23016 Mill Creek Road
Laguna Hills, CA 92654
(714) 859–4040

Society of Manufacturers'
Representatives
30555 Southfield Road, Ste. 255
Southfield, MI 48075
(313) 646–3331

Publications

Articles

Daskal, Melvin H."1985 Survey of Sales Agency Annual Expenses," *Agency Sales Magazine*, April 1986, p. 25.

Daskal, Melvin H., "The First Annual Daskal/SpectorAccountancy Survey of Manufacturers' Sales Agencies for Years 1985-1986," *MANA Research Bulletin*, No. 648, January 1987.

Daskal, Melvin H., "Valuation and Sale of Your Agency Business,"*MANA Bulletin*, No. 105.

"Survey of Sales Commissions Agents Report that Commissions Have Stabilized," *MANA Research Bulletin*, No. 501, June 1985.

"1984 Profile of the Manufacturer's Sales Agency," *MANA Research Bulletin*, No. 535, October 1984.

Books and Pamphlets

Almanac of Business and Industrial Financial Ratios, Prentice-Hall, Englewood Cliffs, N.J., 1986.

Annual Statement Studies, Robert Morris Associates, Philadelphia, 1986.

Daskal, Melvin H., *How to Buy or Sell a Manufacturers' Sales Agency,* Manufacturers' Agents National Association, Laguna Hills, 1983.

Trade Journals

Agency Sales Magazine
Manufacturers' Agents
National Association
23016 Mill Creek Road
Laguna Hills, CA 92654
(714) 859–4040

Sales and Marketing Management
633 3rd Avenue
New York, NY 10017
(212) 986–4800

27

Newspapers, Weekly

Business Description (SIC No. 2711)

Weekly newspapers primarily engage in publishing weekly
newspapers or in printing and publishing weekly newspapers.

Valuation Formula

The publishing industry recognizes two market-derived formulas
useful in the valuation of a weekly newspaper. These formulas are
based on multiples of net revenue and net profit.

Net Revenue Formula

Application of the net revenue formula calls for a multiple of the most
recent 12 months of net revenue. Factors range between 80 percent
and 130 percent, with 100 percent being typical. A multiplier of 105
percent or less should be used if the newspaper produces its own
camera-ready copy, but has the paper printed by another entity. If the
newspaper owns its own printing press, a multiplier in the higher end
of the range should be used. The resulting number indicates the value
of intangible assets, such as goodwill, and fixed assets, exclusive of
real property.

Net Operating Profit Formula

Application of the net operating profit formula requires the use of the most recent annual net profit. The net profit is then multiplied by a factor of between 6 and 12. If after-tax net profits are used, a multiplier of between 9 and 12 should be applied. If the net profit before income taxes is used, a multiplier between 6 and 9 would be appropriate. The resulting value is specifically for intangible and fixed assets, exclusive of real property.

Net Equity Value

To estimate equity value, the value of net current assets, restated at market values less liabilities, is added to the value indicated by the use of the multiplier.

Valuation Considerations

Factors that should be considered when selecting an appropriate multiplier are location, demographic variables, local economic conditions, competition, and lease terms.

Location

The community that the newspaper serves is the most important consideration in the valuation process. The following questions should be answered for a thorough assessment of the community.

1. What is the appearance of the town and stores?
2. What is the condition of the public facilities and the school system?
3. Is there a small college in the community?
4. What is the condition of the community government?
5. Are there good recreational facilities or a major tourist attraction within the town?
6. Is the town on a federal interstate highway?
7. Is the town near a commercial airport?
8. Is there a major shopping center in the community?

Demographic Variables

Demographics such as population density, age, ethnic distribution, and average household income of the surrounding community should be analyzed to predict future revenue potential and associated risk factors. Factors that should be considered include: the volatility of the community population and the county population; community growth in relation to nearby towns; shifts in the age distribution and changes in average household income. A community with a stable or growing population base would tend to receive a multiplier in the high end of the range.

Local Economic Conditions

The local economy should be analyzed for stability and potential community growth. Following are examples of the types of questions that should be investigated.

1. Is the area agricultural, industrial or fuel-oriented?
2. What is the purchasing power and per capita income?
3. Are bank and savings and loan deposits above or below the national average for the local per capita income level?
4. How does the town compare on total retail sales?
5. How do property taxes compare?
6. What is the area's employment rate?

A newspaper located in a community with an expanding economy would tend to receive a multiplier in the higher end of the range.

Competition

Competition within the community is also one of the revealing factors in regard to value. All media sources that sell advertising space or time should be examined. Local radio and television stations should be assessed for market coverage. Newspaper competition should be evaluated by longevity, reputation, circulation, quality of product and total market coverage. If there is a competing newspaper within 15 miles that carries the level of advertising carried by the subject paper, the value of the subject business could decrease by as much as 25–50 percent. The following list contains other questions that should be investigated.

1. Does the competition carry a shopper section (a pull-out section containing advertisements only)?
2. How are the competitive newspapers distributed?
3. Is the subject newspaper locally, regionally, or nationally owned?

Lease Terms

In valuing any small business, consideration should be given to the existing lease terms. The following items are important to consider in regard to lease arrangements: amount of monthly rent, right to sub-lease, and responsibility for utilities and other expenses. A long-term lease with an option to renew would add considerably to the value of a newspaper business.

Example 213

Example

Step 1: Review and make a comparative analysis of income and expense for the previous three years.

Income and Expense Summary
for 12 months ending June 30

	19x6	19x7	19x8
Net Revenue	$731,506	$790,242	$876,338
Cost of Sales	409,643	442,535	484,749
Gross Profit	321,863	347,707	391,589
Operating Expenses	268,703	301,082	303,884
Net Operating Profit*	$ 53,160	$ 46,625	$ 87,705

* Depreciation, excessive owner compensation, and interest added back.

Note: It is important to consider income and expense trends as well as the current year's (19x8) data. To more accurately predict future economic trends, the valuator should review the most recent five years of financial data.

Step 2: Adjust the balance sheet to reflect the market value of tangible assets.

Balance Sheet Summary
as of June 30

	19x6	19x7	19x8	Restated at Market Value on Value Date
Assets				
Current Assets:				
Cash	$ 24,258	$ 28,468	$ 34,542	$ 34,542
Accounts Receivable	72,373	81,321	87,739	80,354
Inventory	7,332	7,996	8,209	8,209
Total Current Assets	103,963	117,785	130,490	123,105
Fixed Assets:				
Trade Fixtures, Leasehold Improvements, and Equipment (net)	73,344	66,415	60,967	115,350
Total Assets	177,307	184,200	191,457	238,455
Liabilities	81,665	74,650	70,930	70,930
Net Tangible Equity	$ 95,642	$109,550	$120,527	$167,525

Step 3: Apply the formulas.

Formula Valuation Using Net Revenue Formula

Net Revenue (Fiscal year end 6/30/x8)	$876,338
Multiplier	× 100%
Indicated Value of Fixed Assets and Intangibles	876,338
Plus Adjusted Market Value of Current Assets	123,105
Total Gross Value	999,443
Less Liabilities	70,930
Net Equity Value	$928,513

Formula Valuation Using Net Operating Profit Formula

Net Operating Profit (Fiscal year end 6/30/x8)	$ 87,705
Annual Multiplier	× 9
Indicated Value of Fixed Assets and Intangibles	789,345
Plus Adjusted Market Value of Current Assets	123,105
Total Gross Value	912,450
Less Liabilities	70,930
Net Equity Value	$841,520

Sources of Further Information

Associations

The National Newspaper Association
1627 K Street, N.W.
Washington, DC 20006
(202) 466–7200

Publications

Article

"How to Determine the Worth of Your Newspaper," *Publishers' Auxiliary,* December 15, 1986, p. 11.

Books and Pamphlets

Almanac of Business and Industrial Financial Ratios, Prentice-Hall, Englewood Cliffs, N.J., 1986.
Annual Statement Studies, Robert Morris Associates, Philadelphia, 1986.

Trade Journals

Editor & Publisher
11 West 19th Street
New York, NY 10011
(212) 675–4380

Publishers' Auxiliary
1627 K Street, N.W
Washington, DC 20006
(202) 466–7200

28

Optometric Practices

Business Description   (SIC No. 8042)

Optometric practices primarily engage in examining eyes for defects and faults of refraction and prescribing correctional lenses or exercises. They do not prescribe drugs or perform surgery.

Valuation Formulas

Three market-derived multiplier formulas are used within the optometric profession to estimate the value of a practice. These are based on multiples of net operating profit and net revenue.

Net Operating Profit Formulas

There are two net operating profit formulas; one for obtaining the value of the practice goodwill and another for valuing the total business, including fixed and intangible assets. When valuing practice goodwill, a multiple ranging from .40 to 1.00 should be applied to the net operating profit. Multiples of .50 to .75 are most common.

To value the fixed and intangible value of an optometric practice, a multiple ranging from 1.5 to 2 should be applied to the net operating profit. If the net profit from the most recent 12 months cannot be considered normal, an average of the most recent 24 to 36 months may be used in either formula. The net operating profit is generally between 30 percent and 40 percent of gross income.

Net Revenue Formula

The net revenue formula utilizes the average of the most recent three years of net revenue. A multiple ranging from .55 to .65 should be applied to the three-year average. The resulting value is for normal amounts of trade fixtures, equipment, and intangible assets.

Net Equity Value

In order to value the total business equity, current assets including cash, inventory, and accounts receivable should be restated at market value and added to the fixed and intangible asset value indicated by the use of the formulas. Liabilities should then be deducted.

Valuation Considerations

Factors that must be considered when valuing an optometric practice include transferability, location and demographics, patient characteristics, quality of management, and lease terms.

Transferability

The ease of transferability of practice ownership and the probable retention of patients is of primary importance in establishing value. Profitability of a practice is closely tied to individual skills, personal patient relations, and productivity. In determining value, the following questions must be answered.

1. Is the seller willing to stay with the practice as a consultant for at least six months?
2. Will the seller provide a letter of introduction for distribution to the patients?
3. What is the probability of staff retention?
4. Will the seller sign a covenant not to compete?
5. Will Preferred Provider Organization contracts transfer to a new owner?

Favorable answers to the above questions as well as a stable profit history would indicate the use of a multiplier in the higher end of the range.

Location and Demographics

Because location is often the key factor in market demand for a practice, a review of the surrounding community is essential. The following questions should be addressed for a thorough locational analysis.

1. Is the surrounding area growing and viable?
2. Is the area's economy sound? Is it capable of growth?
3. How competitive is the community for professionals in this type of practice?
4. What is the area's social makeup?
5. What is the quality of the area's medical services? Transportation systems? School systems?
6. What is the average age within the surrounding community? (Patients over forty have more optometric needs.)

The doctor/patient ratio should also be examined. This ratio can be obtained by dividing the number of optometrists and ophthalmologists who provide optometric services into the area's draw population. According to one industry expert, the doctor/patient ratio should generally average 1:9,000. A ratio under or over this norm would affect the multiplier either positively or negatively.

Patient Characteristics

The characteristics of the active patients should be analyzed to assess the stability of the client following and their future optometric needs. The percentage of patients with private medical insurance and Medicaid, their longevity with the practice, and frequency of visits should be assessed. Consideration should also be given to the percentage of clientele wearing contact lenses and the average age and household income of the patients. These factors will help to measure future revenue potential.

Quality of Management

The quality of the management has a substantial effect on the practice value. This would include marketing, patient recall response, and assistant training as well as payment philosophy, collection history, staff turnover rate, and competitiveness of fees. A practice with a well-trained staff, high fees, and patient satisfaction would tend to command a multiplier in the higher end of the range.

Lease Terms

In valuing any small business, consideration should be given to the existing lease terms for the real property. The following items are important considerations in analyzing lease arrangements: the amount of monthly rent, the right to sublease, and the responsibility for maintenance, taxes, insurance, and other property expenses. A long-term lease with an option to renew would add considerably to the value of an optometric practice.

Example 221

Example

Step 1: Review and make a comparative analysis of income and expense for the previous three years.

Income and Expense Summary
for 12 months ending June 30

	19x6	19x7	19x8
Net Revenue	$168,283	$188,463	$201,329
Operating Expenses	113,443	121,979	128,581
Net Operating Profit*	$ 54,840	$ 66,484	$ 72,748

* Depreciation, excessive owner compensation, and interest added back.

Note: It is important to consider income and expense trends as well as the current year's
(19x8) data. To more accurately predict future economic trends, the valuator should review
the most recent five years of financial data.

Step 2: Adjust the balance sheet to reflect market value of tangible assets.

Balance Sheet Summary
as of June 30

	19x6	19x7	19x8	Restated at Market Value on Value Date
Assets				
Current Assets:				
Cash	$ 27,486	$ 32,484	$ 39,500	$ 39,500
Accounts Receivable	9,852	10,985	11,483	10,909
Inventory	8,593	9,837	9,573	8,950
Total Current Assets	45,931	53,306	60,556	59,359
Fixed Assets:				
Trade Fixtures,				
Leasehold Improvements,				
and Equipment	38,950	32,585	28,500	36,500
Total Assets	84,881	85,891	89,056	95,859
Liabilities	21,847	18,993	25,837	25,837
Net Tangible Equity	$ 63,034	$ 66,898	$ 63,219	$ 70,022

Step 3: Apply the formulas.

Formula Valuation Using Net Operating Profit for Goodwill Value

Net Operating Profit (Fiscal year end 6/30/x8)	$ 72,748
Multiplier	×____.75
Indicated Value of Goodwill	$ 54,561

Formula Valuation Using Net Operating Profit For Fixed and Intangible Value

Net Operating Profit (Fiscal year end 06/30/x8)	$ 59,847
Multiplier	×___1.75
Indicated Value of Fixed Assets and Intangibles	104,732
Plus Adjusted Market Value of Current Assets	59,359
Total Gross Value	164,091
Less Liabilities	25,837
Net Equity Value	$138,254

Formula Valuation Using Annual Net Revenue

Three-year Average of Net Revenue	$186,025
Multiplier	×____.60
Indicated Value of Fixed Assets and Intangibles	111,615
Plus Adjusted Market Value of Current Assets	59,359
Total Gross Value	170,974
Less Liabilities	25,837
Net Equity Value	$145,137

Sources of Further Information

Associations

American Academy of Optometry
5530 Wisconsin Avenue, N.W.
Suite 950
Washington, DC 20815
(301) 652–0905

National Association of
Optometrists & Opticians
18903 South Miles Road
Cleveland, OH 44128
(216) 475–8925

American Optometric Association
243 North Lindberg Boulevard
St. Louis, MO 63141
(314) 991–4100

Publications

Articles

Gregg, James R.,"Your Practice Profile: Net Worth," *Optometric Management*, May 1981, pp. 45–53.

Hubler, Richard S., "A New Approach to Evaluating the Worth of a Practice," *Optometric Management*, March 1987, pp. 40, 42, 44.

Hubler, Richard S., "How to Buy (or Maybe Sell) an Optometric Practice," *Optometric Management*, May 1982, pp. 27–32.

Levy, Jerome T., "Don't Sell Your Practice Short," *Optometric Management*, January 1986, pp. 49–52.

Mashioff, Lorraine, "The Great News About Goodwill," *Optometric Management*, February 1980, pp. 69, 71, 73, 75.

Petrie, Kurt J., "Evaluating the Worth of a Practice," *Optometric Management*, November 1986, pp. 18–19.

Phipps, Richard F.,"Facts About Buying and Selling All or Part of an Optometric Practice," *Journal of the Missouri Optometric Association,* First Quarter 1983, pp. 17–22.

"Selling Your Solo Practice," *Review of Optometry*, December 1984, p. 20.

Thal, Lawrence S., "The Practice Sale: Getting to the Bottom Line," *Optometric Management*, June 1986, pp. 66–67.

Books and Pamphlets

Almanac of Business and Industrial Financial Ratios, Prentice-Hall, Englewood Cliffs, N.J., 1986.

Annual Statement Studies, Robert Morris Associates, Philadelphia, 1986.

General Guidelines for Buying/Selling and Establishing the Worth of an Optometric Practice,. American Optometric Association. (No date).

Trade Journals

American Optometric News
American Optometric Association
243 North Lindberg Boulevard
St. Louis, MO 63141
(314) 991–4100

Optometric Management
Four Ansley Medical Park
1013 North Fifth Avenue
Rome, GA 30161
(404) 291–4650

20/20
Jobson Publishing Corporation
352 Park Avenue South
New York, NY 10010
(212) 685–4848

29

Print Shops, Commercial

Business Description   (SIC No. 2751)

Print shops primarily engage in letterpress and screen commercial or
job printing, including flexgraphic. This industry includes general
print shops as well as shops specializing in printing newspapers and
periodicals for others and those who specialize in screen printing.

Valuation Formulas

Two market derived formulas are useful in the valuation of a small
commercial print shop. These formulas are based on multiples of
monthly net sales and net operating profit.

Monthly Net Sales Formula

The monthly net sales formula uses the average monthly net sales
from the latest 12-month period. Multipliers range from 4 to 8, with
5 and 6 being typical. The resulting value allows for normal amounts
of trade fixtures and equipment, leasehold improvements, and intangible value.

Net Operating Profit Formula

The net operating profit formula applies a multiple to the net operating income from the most recent 12-month period. Multipliers typically range from 4 to 6. The value indicated by the use of the multiplier is for fixed assets and intangibles.

Net Equity Value

In order to value the total business equity, current assets including cash, inventory, and accounts receivable should be restated at market value and added to the intangible and fixed asset value indicated by the use of the formulas. Liabilities to be assumed should then be deducted.

Valuation Considerations

Factors that should be considered when valuing a small commercial print shop include location, reputation, client mix, condition of facility and equipment, and lease terms.

Location

The two most important locational components for a small print shop are accessibility and visibility. Small commercial print shops and quick print shops cater to the walk-in client who needs a small job done in a hurry. Street front sites in downtown office districts close to customers and trade services are considered the most desirable locations. The site should have parking available for customers and employees and room for expansion for the next three to five years.

Larger print shops that specialize in more complex jobs may find a street front location distracting. Larger printers cannot handle walk-in patrons because their requests are often small, infrequent, and sometimes needed too quickly. A less central location, where property is less expensive, with ample loading and parking space would be optimal.

Reputation

Because the printing business is highly competitive, it is imperative for the valuator to investigate the reputation of the shop. The quality of service, the finished product, and timeliness of delivery should all be scrutinized.

The shop's reputation of consistency and competitiveness of prices can be an indicator of the quality of management. It is not uncommon for potential customers as well as established patrons to solicit several estimates on printing jobs. A history of pricing first-time jobs below market prices and then hiking prices on recurring jobs would indicate poor shop management and possibly a less than loyal clientele. Past customers can be a revealing source for this type of information.

Client Mix

There should be a balance in the number of customers and accounts that make up the revenue stream. Reliance on any one account would indicate a high risk to future revenues due to client attrition. Generally, no account should comprise more than 10 percent of net revenue. A potential buyer would have to assume the worst, therefore a concentration of accounts could lower the value of the business.

Condition of Facility and Equipment

As with any asset-intensive business, the condition of the existing facility and equipment is extremely important to the business value. All pieces of major equipment should be examined. Any evidence of obsolescence or inadequacy could lower the value of the print shop considerably.

Lease Terms

In valuing any small business, consideration should be given to the existing lease terms. The following items are important to consider in regard to lease arrangements: amount of monthly rent, right to sublease, and responsibility for utilities and other expenses. A long-term lease with an option to renew would add considerably to the value of a shop.

Example

Step 1: Review and make a comparative analysis of income and expense for the previous three years.

Income and Expense Summary
for 12 months ending June 30

	19x6	19x7	19x8
Net Revenue	$412,875	$454,163	$499,579
Cost of Sales	227,081	249,790	274,768
Gross Profit	185,794	204,373	224,811
Operating Expenses	144,506	158,957	174,853
Net Operating Profit*	$ 41,288	$ 45,416	$ 49,958

* Depreciation, excessive owner compensation, and interest added back.

Note: It is important to consider income and expense trends as well as the current year's (19x8) data. To more accurately predict future economic trends, the valuator should review the most recent five years of financial data.

Step 2: Adjust the balance sheet to reflect the market value of tangible assets.

Balance Sheet Summary
as of June 30

	19x6	19x7	19x8	Restated at Market Value on Value Date
Assets				
Current Assets:				
Cash	$13,483	$14,287	$14,984	$14,984
Accounts Receivable	25,384	28,487	27,343	26,450
Inventory	11,837	13,998	14,873	14,350
Total Current Assets	50,704	56,772	57,200	55,784
Fixed Assets:				
Trade Fixtures, Leasehold Improvements, and Equipment	62,850	56,565	50,280	57,500
Total Assets	113,554	113,337	107,480	113,284
Liabilities	29,453	27,584	25,488	27,488
Net Tangible Equity	$ 84,101	$ 85,753	$ 81,992	$ 85,796

Example 229

Step 3: Apply the formula.

Formula Valuation Using Monthly Net Sales

Annual Net Sales (Fiscal year end 6/30/x8)	$499,579
divided by 12	÷_____12
Monthly Net Sales	41,632
Multiplier	×_____6
Indicated Value of Fixed Assets and Intangibles	249,792
Plus Adjusted Market Value of Current Assets	55,784
Total Gross Value	305,576
Less Liabilities	27,488
Net Equity Value	$278,088

Formula Valuation Using Net Operating Profit

Net Operating Profit (Fiscal year end 6/30/x8)	$ 49,958
Multiplier	×_____5
Indicated Value of Fixed Assets and Intangibles	249,790
Plus Adjusted Market Value of Current Assets	55,784
Total Gross Value	305,574
Less Liabilities	27,488
Net Equity Value	$278,086

Sources of Further Information

Associations

National Association of
Printers and Lithographers
780 Palisade Avenue
Teaneck, NJ 07666
(201) 342–0705

National Printing Equipment
and Supply Association
1889 Preston White Drive
Reston, VA 22091
(703) 734–8285

National Association
of Quick Printers
111 East Wacker Drive, Suite 600
Chicago, IL 60601
(312) 644–6610

Printing Industries of America
1730 North Lynn Street
Arlington, VA 22209
(703) 841–8100

Publications

Books and Pamphlets

Almanac of Business and Industrial Financial Ratios, Prentice-Hall,
Englewood Cliffs, N.J., 1986.
Annual Statement Studies, Robert Morris Associates, Philadelphia,
1986.
Hunt, Larry, *How Much Is Your Printing Business Worth*, Tampa
Bay, FL, 1982.

Trade Journals

American Printers Magazine
Maclean Hunter
Publishing Corporation
300 West Adams Street
Chicago, IL 60606
(312) 726–2802

Instant Printing Magazine
Innes Publishing
425 Huehl Road
Northbrook, IL 60062
(312) 564–5940

Printing Impressions
North American
Publishing Company
401 North Broad Street
Philadelphia, PA 19108
(215) 238–5300

Quick Printing Magazine
Coast Publishing
1680 Southwest Bayshore Blvd.
Port St. Lucy, FL 34984
(305) 879–6666

30

Real Estate Agencies

Business Description   (SIC No. 6531)

Real estate agencies primarily lease, buy and sell real estate for others.

Valuation Formula

Real estate agencies are commonly valued by a multiple of net operating profit plus fair market value of fixed assets. Net operating profit multipliers generally range between 1 and 2, with 1.5 being typical. The multiplier primarily depends on internal factors such as continuity of personnel, market share, and historic earnings and external factors such as interest rates, economic outlook, and demographic trends.

Net Equity Value

In order to value the total business equity, current assets including cash and accounts receivable should be restated at market value and added to the intangible and fixed asset value indicated by the use of the formula. Liabilities should then be deducted.

Valuation Considerations

Factors that should be considered when valuing a real estate agency include quality and retention of salespeople, owner compensation, size of the company, demographic and external variables, current listings, pending sales, and lease terms.

Salespeople

It is necessary to review the production profile of each salesperson, current and past, to serve as an indication of future performance. Factors to consider for each individual salesperson include listings, sales, and contributions during the past years, aptitude, experience, potential, motivation, and the likelihood of the firm retaining the salesperson. If, after the analysis, it is determined that the core of the sales staff comprises experienced full-time salespeople who have been affiliated with the company for three or more years and who consistently contribute the greater percentage of production, a multiplier in the higher end of the range should be applied.

Owner Compensation

When using a net operating profit multiplier, it is essential to establish how the owner is compensated for his or her contribution to the firm. This is not always obvious from a review of financial statements due to the commission basis typical within the real estate industry. If the owner is actively selling, he or she should be receiving part of the commissions. If the owner is actively selling but is not participating in the commissions, it must be established what he or she could make fulfilling the same role (without ownership) in another company. Any adjustments for over- or under-compensation must be made before applying the multiplier.

Size of the Company

It is not uncommon for small agencies to sell for their net asset value. Smaller firms are very dependent on the owner or a few key sales personnel. When they leave, literally all that is left are empty desks and chairs. In this instance, intangible assets such as reputation and going concern have little or no value.

On the other hand, medium- and large-sized firms do not depend entirely on the owner but rely on support personnel and the sales staff as well . A real estate agency of this size will be able to withstand a transfer of ownership and probably has considerable intangible value.

Demographic Trends and External Factors

Demographic factors, including population migration, age distribution of the population, and income distribution, can directly affect sales. A higher proportion of residents in the 25- to 44-year-old age group in a community might lead to more home sales in that area than in an area where the population is much older, for example. Or, if the average income in a geographic area is lower than in another, there may not be fewer sales, but the average home price will be less. If the agency specializes in commercial and industrial sales, the vacancy rates and business indicators in the area should be assessed. Other demographic and external factors that should be assessed include

— development within the community
— competition and market share
— general economic trends including inflation
—mortgage interest rates (higher, long-term rates mean lower firm values)

Demographic and external factors will have an impact on local real estate firm earnings over a relatively longer period of time (such as the population shift to the South and West) which can ultimately affect the firm's value.

Current Listings

A firm usually obtains listings of numerous properties for sale . Many of these active listings should lease or eventually sell. Listings, like pending sales or leases, represent potential income to the firm. The valuator should consider active listings in the valuation process if the firm plans to continue operating as it had in the past. Value the firm's listings by considering list prices, probability of selling, age of listing, exclusivity, and historical operating results. The listings can be assessed either collectively or individually, with adjustments for the probability of split commissions.

Pending Sales

One or more sales in a firm are usually pending closing. Because they
represent contingent income and, thus, contingent cash, pending sales
should be valued and included in an ongoing firm's value. Pending
sales should be valued by using contract information, probability of
closing, and historical operating data.

Lease Terms

In valuing any small business, consideration should be given to the
existing lease terms. The following items are important to consider
in regard to lease arrangements: amount of monthly rent, right to sublease, and responsibility for utilities and other expenses. A long-term
lease with an option to renew would add considerably to the value of
a brokerage.

Example 237

Example

Step 1: Review and make a comparative analysis of income and expense for the previous
three years.

Income and Expense Summary
for 12 months ending June 30

	19x6	19x7	19x8
Net Revenue	$708,959	$744,407	$781,627
Commission Payout	427,174	448,533	470,959
Company Dollar	281,785	295,874	310,668
Operating Expenses	248,881	257,145	270,281
Net Operating Profit*	$ 34,904	$ 38,729	$ 40,387

* Depreciation, excessive owner compensation, and interest added back.

Note: It is important to consider income and expense trends as well as the current year's
(19x8) data. To more accurately predict future economic trends, the valuator should review
the most recent five years of financial data.

Step 2: Adjust the balance sheet to reflect the market value of tangible assets.

Balance Sheet Summary
as of June 30

	19x6	19x7	19x8	Restated at Market Value on Value Date
Assets				
Current Assets:				
Cash	$13,483	$21,532	$22,561	$22,561
Accounts Receivable	11,532	15,131	16,883	16,375
Total Current Assets	25,015	36,663	39,444	38,936
Fixed Assets:				
Trade Fixtures, Leasehold Improvements, and Equipment	29,108	25,311	20,001	24,775
Total Assets	54,123	61,974	59,445	63,711
Liabilities	12,591	10,825	8,210	8,210
Net Tangible Equity	$ 41,532	$ 51,149	$ 51,235	$ 55,501

Step 3: Apply the formula.

Formula Valuation Using Net Operating Profit

Net Operating Profit (Fiscal year end 06/30/x8)	$ 40,387
Multiplier	× 1.50
Indicated Value of Intangibles Assets	60,580
Plus Adjusted Market Value of Tangible Assets	
Current	38,936
Fixed	24,775
Total Gross Value	124,291
Less Liabilities	8,210
Net Equity Value	$116,081

Sources of Further Information

Associations

National Association of
Real Estate Brokers
1101 14th Street, N.W., Suite 900
Washington, DC 20005
(202) 289–6655

National Association
of Realtors
430 North Michigan Avenue
Chicago, IL 60611
(312) 329–8200

Publications

Articles

Brown, James ,"Your Brokerage Firm: What Is Its Value," *Real Estate Business*, Spring 1985, pp. 29–33.

Epley, Donald R., and Warren Banks, "The Pricing of Real Estate Brokerage for Services Actually Offered," *Real Estate Issues,* Spring/Summer 1985, pp 45–51.

"How to Negotiate the Purchase of a Real Estate Office," *Real Estate Insider Weekly Newsletter*, August 22, 1977.

"Sales Price of a Real Estate Office Should Be Value of its Assets," *Real Estate Insider Weekly Newsletter*, October 1977.

"Sales Value of Real Estate Office One to Three Times Annual Net Cash Flow," *Real Estate Insider Weekly Newsletter,* August 29, 1977.

"There Is No Set Formula for Buying a Real Estate Firm," *Real Estate Insider Weekly Newsletter,* August 15, 1977.

Books and Pamphlets

Almanac of Business and Industrial Financial Ratios, Prentice-Hall, Englewood, N.J., 1986.

Annual Statement Studies, Robert Morris Associates, Philadelphia, 1986.

Inside the Real Estate Business, The National Association of Realtors, Chicago, 1982.

Real Estate Brokerage 1985— Income, Expenses, Profits, Real Estate Business Series, National Association of Realtors, Chicago, 1985.

Real Estate Office Management People Functions Systems, National Association of Realtors, Chicago, 1975.

Value of a Brokerage Firm, National Association of Realtors, Chicago, 1978.

Trade Journals

Real Estate Today
National Association of Realtors
430 North Michigan Avenue
Chicago, IL 60611
(312) 329–8200

Real Estate Insider
Weekly Newsletter
Atcom, Inc.
2315 Broadway
New York, NY 10024
(212) 873–5900

Real Estate Business
Realtors' National
Marketing Institute
430 North Michigan Avenue
Chicago, IL 60611
(312) 329–8200

Real Estate Issues
American Society of
Real Estate Councilors
430 North Michigan Avenue
Chicago, IL 60611
(312) 329–8257

31

Travel Agencies

Business Description   (SIC No. 4722)

Travel agencies primarily engage in furnishing travel information, acting as agents in arranging tours and transportation for passengers, and acting as independent ticket agencies for transportation companies.

Valuation Formulas

The travel agency industry recognizes two market-derived formulas for developing the value of an agency. These techniques are the net revenue formula and the net commissions formula.

Net Revenue Formula

Value multipliers for the net revenue formula range from 4 percent to 10 percent of net revenue, with 6 percent to 7 percent being most common. The total indicated value resulting from the use of the net sales formula includes trade fixtures, equipment, and all intangible assets, including goodwill. The multiplier percentage used for a travel agency depends on such factors as the agency's accreditation, source of income, staff experience, and location.

Net Commissions Formula

In developing value based on the percentage of net commissions, all sources of travel agency income are considered. Value multipliers for this method range between 60 percent and 70 percent of net commissions. The average commission rate for travel agency sales is 10 percent. Therefore, the net commissions method closely parallels the net sales formula, with the value multiplier for the former method being approximately 10 times the multiplier used in the latter method. The value resulting from the use of the net commissions formula includes normal levels of fixtures and equipment and intangibles, such as goodwill.

Net Equity Value

To estimate equity value, the value of net current assets, restated at market values less liabilities, is added to the value indicated by the use of the multiplier.

Valuation Considerations

Two factors have contributed to a recent decrease in agency revenues: airline deregulation and the dynamic nature of world events. Airline deregulation greatly depressed airline revenues by increasing competition, which served to lower flight prices to passengers. This caused a decrease in agency commissions of nearly 10 percent from the first half of 1985, when deregulation took full effect, to mid-1986. In addition, current world events, such as the recent rise in terrorism, have deterred European travel and further depressed agency revenues. This decrease in commissions, coupled with increased labor costs has had a disastrous effect on travel agency profits, resulting in a reduction in the value of travel agency businesses. The valuator should consider current trends and conditions in the industry as well as international political conditions at the time of valuation.

Other factors that must be considered in the valuation process include accreditation, transferability, revenue mix, location, and lease terms.

Accreditation

Although accreditation is no longer necessary for the operation of a travel agency, it is preferable. The agent designation CTC (Certified Travel Counselor) and agency accreditation by the ARC (Airline Reporting Corporation) can increase the value of an agency not only by establishing the business' professionalism, but also by allowing the agency to use standard ticket stock and hold a multilateral agreement with the airlines. An agency that has a qualified, accredited staff can often command a higher multiplier than an agency that is unable to meet the accreditation requirements.

When valuing a travel agency for purchase or sale, it is important to realize that agency accreditations are not automatically transferable to a new owner. The new owner must reapply and meet the requirements imposed on a new agency. To receive accreditation an agency must meet specific financial standards in addition to bonding, personnel, and location requirements.

Transferability

In the purchase of travel agencies, it is general practice for the owner or key employee to remain with the new agency for a period of time. This practice tends to ease the complications of agency transfer, particularly by allowing for an introduction of existing clients to the buyer. If the seller or key employee does not remain, it is important to review the percentage of net commissions serviced by the remaining staff and to evaluate the probability of their retention. The valuator should also examine the qualifications and accreditation of the staff. An agency fortunate enough to possess a qualified staff, with a high probability of staff retention, would receive a multiplier in the higher end of the range.

Commercial versus Leisure Accounts

In analyzing an agency, the valuator should understand the different risks, revenue potential, and cash flow problems associated with specialization and revenue mix. For example, major national agencies are capturing a larger percentage of corporate accounts than smaller independent agencies, making it increasingly risky for small agencies to specialize in and compete for business accounts. Most commercial accounts bill and pay at the end of the month. Obviously, this can cause a severe cash flow problem if a majority of the accounts are businesses. Leisure travelers, on the other hand, normally pay a substantial deposit 30 to 45 days in advance of their departure. Most experts recommend a balance of commercial and leisure accounts to minimize cash flow problems. If there is a balanced mix of active accounts, the cash flow problem can be eliminated.

Location

A further consideration in valuing a travel agency is location. The valuator should analyze whether the location of the agency is appropriate for its specialization. Agencies that specialize in business travel thrive in business districts, particularly on the ground level of large office complexes. However, a leisure travel agency could easily fail in the same location. Agencies specializing in pleasure travel are most profitable in suburban areas, either in a highly visible street store front or in a shopping mall. It should be emphasized that lease costs in shopping malls may be too expensive for the low profit margins of travel agencies.

Lease Terms

In valuing any small business, consideration should be given to the existing lease terms. The following items are important to consider in regard to lease arrangements: amount of monthly rent, right to sublease, and lessee responsibility for utilities and other expenses. A long-term lease with an option to renew would add considerably to the value of an agency.

Example 245

Example

Step 1: Review and make a comparative analysis of income and expense for the last three years.

Income and Expense Summary
for 12 months ending June 30

	19x6	19x7	19x8
Net Revenue	$1,343,824	$1,298,680	$1,385,679
Net Commissions	130,351	125,972	134,411
Operating Expenses	114,593	119,354	123,247
Net Operating Profit*	$ 15,758	$ 6,618	$ 11,164

* Depreciation, excessive owner compensation, and interest added back.

Note: It is important to consider income and expense trends as well as the current year's (19x8) data. To more accurately predict future economic trends, the valuator should review the most recent five years of financial data.

Step 2: Adjust the balance sheet to reflect the market value of tangible assets.

Balance Sheet Summary
as of June 30

	19x6	19x7	19x8	Restated at Market Value on Value Date
Assets				
Current Assets:				
Cash	$ 15,847	$ 14,184	$ 16,146	$ 16,146
Accounts receivable	18,211	19,730	22,187	20,859
Total Current Assets	34,058	33,914	38,333	37,005
Fixed Assets:				
Trade Fixtures, Leasehold Improvements, and Equipment (net)	14,002	13,458	14,089	17,960
Total Assets	48,060	47,372	52,422	54,965
Liabilities	7,329	6,840	11,578	11,578
Net Tangible Equity	$ 40,731	$ 40,532	$ 40,844	$ 43,387

Step 3: Apply the formulas.

Formula Valuation Using Annual Net Revenue Multiplier

Annual Net Revenue (Fiscal year end 6/30/x8)	$1,385,679
Annual Multiplier	× 7%
Indicated Value of Fixed Assets and Intangibles	96,998
Plus Adjusted Market Value of Current Assets	37,005
Total Gross Value	134,003
Less Liabilities	11,578
Net Equity Value	$ 122,425

Formula Valuation Using Net Commissions Multiplier

Net Commissions (Fiscal year end 6/30/x8)	$134,411
Annual Multiplier	× 70%
Indicated Value of Fixed Assets and Intangibles	94,088
Plus Adjusted Market Value of Current Assets	37,005
Total Gross Value	131,093
Less Liabilities	11,578
Net Equity Value	$119,515

Sources of Further Information

Associations

American Society of Travel Agents
1101 King Street, Suite 200
Alexandria, DC 22314
(703) 739–2782

Institute of Certified
Travel Agents
148 Linden Street
Wellesley, MA 02181
(617) 237–0280

Accreditor

Airline Reporting Corporation
1709 New York Avenue, NW
Washington, DC 20006
(202) 626–4079

Publications

Article

Sontag, Peter, "Pinning Down the Worth of a Firm," *Travel Weekly,*
August, 1980.

Books and Pamphlets

Almanac of Business and Industrial Financial Ratios, Prentice-Hall,
Englewood Cliffs, N.J., 1986.
Annual Statement Studies, Robert Morris Associates, Philadelphia,
1986.
Gove, Larry W., *Travel Agency for Sale, A Purchaser's Guide,* In-
stitute of Certified Travel Agents, Wellesley, Mass.,July 1985.
McCurdy, Chuck, *So You Want To Buy a Travel Agency?,*Institute
of Ceritified Travel Agents, Wellesley, Mass. April 1985.
Stevens, Laurenc*e, Guide to Starting and Operating a Successful
Travel Agency,* Merton House Travel and Tourism Publishers,
Wheaton, Ill., 1983.

Trade Journals

Travel Age East
888 7th Avenue
New York, NY 10106
(212) 977–8310

Travel Weekly
1 Park Avenue
New York, NY 10016
(212) 503–3600

Travel Agent
2 West 46th Street
New York, NY 10036
(212) 575–9000

32

Veterinary Practices

Business Description   (SIC No. 0742)

Veterinary practices comprise licensed practitioners who practice veterinary medicine, dentistry, or surgery, for animal specialties. Animal specialties include horses, bees, fish, fur-bearing animals, rabbits, dogs, cats, and other pets, and birds, except poultry. This category also includes animal hospitals.

Valuation Formula

Valuation formulas for veterinary practices generally are based on a multiple of the most current 12 months of net revenue. The net revenue multiplier typically ranges from .75 to 1.5, with .90 being typical. If the latest 12 months cannot be considered normal, a 12-month average based on the proceeding 24 to 36 months may be used. This valuation formula results in an indicated value for the intangible value of the practice, including goodwill.

Net Equity Value

To estimate equity value, the value of net current assets, restated at market values less liabilities, is added to the value indicated by the use of the multiplier.

Valuation Considerations

Among the factors that must be considered when selecting a multiplier are the type and transferability of the practice, demographic variables, location, and lease terms.

Practice Type and Transferability

Practice type and potential ease of transferability are highly correlated. Equine and large-animal practices have different transferability complications than do small-animal practices, therefore, special considerations must be taken in valuing each.

Equine and large-animal practices rely heavily on personal contacts, referrals, and a long-standing reputation. Because of the exceptionally personal nature of this type of specialty, the goodwill is often within the veterinarian, making the practice difficult to sell as a going concern. If the client referrals cannot be transferred to a buyer, the practice may have limited intangible value, and a multiplier in the lower end of the range would be applicable. However, if the practitioner agrees to stay with the practice for an extended period of time subsequent to the sale and signs a covenant not to compete, the practice may have transferable goodwill.

A small-animal practice is more easily transferred to a new owner. Small-animal practices normally take one of three forms: a one-person clinic with limited overnight facilities; a two-person hospital often with overnight facilities; or a group practice with partners pooling specialties to offer a full-service animal hospital. Each type must be scrutinized for ease of transferability. As with large-animal practices, one-person clinics may have limited transferable intangible value. Two-person and group practices tend to have a lower risk of decreased future revenues as partners and associates may help to ease the transfer. This can make it easier for the buyer to retain existing earnings levels. However, it is still important for the seller to remain with the practice for up to six months subsequent to the sale and to sign a covenant not to compete in order to apply a multiplier in the higher end of the range.

Demographic Variables

Demographic variables such as population, age, and household income should be reviewed in the valuation analysis. These variables often determine client characteristics and the practice's fee structure.

For example, small-animal practices in middle-to-high income areas tend to have a higher revenue base and fewer problems with receivables than do practices in lower-income areas. This is due to the medical sophistication of the clients and their ability to pay for services when rendered. However, it is important that the facilities be adequate to service the specialized needs of sophisticated clients. Practices in middle-to-high income areas often receive higher-than-average fees, are more attractive to potential buyers, and therefore command multipliers in the higher end of the range.

The age of the population should also be noted. Households with parents between the ages of 20 and 40 who own their own homes tend to have the highest concentration of pets. A trend toward apartments or condominiums in the area could place a potential risk on future revenues for a veterinary practice

Location

The location of the animal hospital within the community is a major consideration. Because of professional ethics, the possibilities for advertising are limited and the most effective advertising for a veterinary practice may be good site exposure. A practice located on a major street that services a rapidly growing residential district could receive a multiplier in the higher end of the range.

Because veterinarians often own the premises from which they operate, a locational analysis should include real property values in the area as well as property tax trends. If the new owner is to purchase the property, the valuator should investigate whether potential income from the business would support such a purchase. Annual taxes should be within a range that the practice would be able to support if sold as a going concern.

Lease Terms

The following items are important to consider in regard to lease arrangements: amount of monthly rent, right to sublease, and lessee responsibility for utilities and other expenses. Because of the specialized nature of veterinarian facilities, it is imperative that the practice have a long term remaining on the lease. A long-term lease with an option to renew would add considerably to the value of a practice.

Relocation could be extremely difficult due to zoning restrictions and the high cost of the necessary leasehold improvements. If the real property is owned by the practitioner, it must be valued separately from the business. In such instances, economic rent is added as an operating expense and interest and depreciation expenses related to the building are deducted from business operating expenses.

Example 253

Example

Step 1: Review and make a comparative analysis of income and expense for the previous
three years.

Income and Expense Summary
for 12 months ending June 30

	19x6	19x7	19x8
Net Revenue	219,231	225,328	244,186
Operating Expenses	207,065	212,815	230,178
Net Operating Profit*	$ 12,166	$ 12,513	$ 14,008

* Depreciation, excessive owner compensation, and interest added back.

Note: It is important to consider income and expense trends as well as the current year's
(19x8) data. To more accurately predict future economic trends, the valuator should review
the most recent five years of financial data.

Step 2: Adjust the balance sheet to reflect the market value of tangible assets.

Balance Sheet Summary
as of June 30

	19x6	19x7	19x8	Restated at Market Value on Value Date
Assets				
Current Assets:				
Cash	$ 21,978	$ 29,816	$ 35,121	$ 35,121
Receivables	13,784	19,390	15,908	14,100
Total Current Assets	35,762	49,206	51,029	49,221
Fixed Assets:				
Trade Fixtures,				
Leasehold Improvements,				
and Equipment (net)	60,975	65,215	60,545	75,350
Total Assets	96,737	114,421	111,574	124,571
Liabilities	78,874	81,672	75,425	75,425
Net Tangible Equity	$ 17,863	$ 32,749	$ 36,149	$ 49,146

Step 3: Apply the formula.

Formula Valuation Using Net Revenue Multiplier

Net Revenue (Fiscal year end 6/30/x8)	$244,186
Annual Multiplier	× .90
Indicated Value of Intangible Assets	219,767
Plus Adjusted Market Value of Tangible Assets	
Current	49,221
Fixed	75,350
Total Gross Value	344,338
Less Liabilities	75,425
Net Equity Value	$268,913

Sources of Further Information

Associations

American Animal Hospital Association
P.O. Box 768
204 Lincolnway East
Mishawaka, IN 46574
(219) 256–0280

American Veterinary Medical Association
930 N. Meacham Road
Schaumburg, IL 60196
(800) 248–2862

Publications

Books and Pamphlets

Almanac of Business and Industrial Financial Ratios, Prentice-Hall, Englewood Cliffs, N.J., 1986.
Annual Statement Studies, Robert Morris Associates, Philadelphia, 1986.
Establishing a Veterinary Practice, Professional Management, Bank of America, San Francisco, 1974.
Your Complete Guide to Setting Practice Fees, Veterinary Medicine Publishing Company, 1985.

Articles

Douglas, Edward P., and Owen E. McCafferty, "Determining Practice Value," *Veterinary Economics*, July 1977, pp. 21–51.
McCafferty, Owen E., "How to Price Your Practice," *Veterinary Economics*, July 1983, pp. 39–50.
McCafferty, Owen E., "How to Price Your Practice—Part 2," *Veterinary Economics*, August 1983, pp. 56–64.
McCafferty, Owen E., "How to Price Your Practice—Part 3," *Veterinary Economics*, September 1983, pp. 68–70.

Trade Journals

Journal of the American
Veterinary Medical Association
930 N. Meacham Road
Schaumburg, IL 60196
(312) 885–8070

Journal of the American
Animal Hospital Association
P.O. Box 1304
Elkhart, IN 46514
(219) 256–0280

Modern Veterinary Practice
American Veterinary
Publications
5782 Thornwood Drive
Goleta, CA 93117-3896
(805) 967–5988

Veterinary Economics
Veterinary Medicine
Publishing Co.
9073 Lenexa Drive
Lenexa, KS 66215
(913) 492-4300

33

Video Rental and Sales Shops

Business Description   (SIC No. 5999)

Video rental and sales shops primarily engage in renting and retail sale of video cassettes for at-home viewing.

Valuation Formula

Valuation formulas for video stores are based on a multiple of the net operating profit. The multiplier generally ranges between 1 and 2, with 1.5 being typical. The resulting value is specifically for the business' intangible assets. Fixed assets such as trade fixtures and equipment must then be restated at market value and added to the intangible asset value indicated by the use of the multiplier.

Net Equity Value

To estimate equity value, the value of net current assets, restated at market values less liabilities, is added to the value indicated by the use of the multiplier.

Valuation Considerations

Among the factors that should be considered when selecting a multiplier are inventory, location, competition, and lease terms.

Video Cassette Inventory

Video cassettes are expensive and can represent a significant portion of the total outlay to open a new video store. It is important, therefore, to evaluate whether or not the tapes are up-to-date and in good condition. Evidence of obsolescence or poor-quality cassette tapes would affect the multiplier negatively.

The inventory should also be assessed for the quality of selection. Is the inventory balanced as to categories of movies (that is, adventure, classic, foreign)? Does the stock fit the customer base? When making this type of assessment, it is important to review the demographics of the surrounding area. Higher-income areas tend to support a larger classics category. In lower-income areas, there is a higher rate of adventure, action and horror movie rentals.

Location

The location of a video store may be an indicator of its future success. Video stores tend to be more successful if located on a major traffic artery with high visibility. The valuator should examine the traffic flow at the site and assess the ease of accessibility and adequacy of parking facilities. Is the store in a business district that is vacated by 5:30 P.M.? (Most video stores have their most profitable hours after 6:00 P.M.) The demographic variables of the surrounding community, such as current and projected population figures and income levels, should also be examined. Is the area primarily suburban, close to apartment buildings and/or single family homes? A video store in a growing suburban community would tend to receive a multiplier in the high end of the range.

Competition

Competition is fierce in the video rental industry. The number of outlets that rent and/or sell video cassettes has surged from as few as 10,000 in 1981 to more than 35,000 in 1987. Presently, mass merchandisers, grocery stores, and a number of other retailers are dispensing video cassettes. When examining the competition, all current and potential video cassette dispensers must be assessed. The products and services offered by the subject business, including size of the video cassette library and appearance of the facilities, should be compared to the competition.

Success within the industry depends on the ingenuity of the proprietor and/or a lack of competition. A video store that occupies an exclusive market niche, such as offering home delivery or drive-through service, is more likely to outlive the competition. A multiplier in the high end of the range would be appropriate for a video store that holds an exclusive market niche along with limited competition.

Lease Terms

In valuing a video store, consideration should be given to the existing lease terms. The following items are important to consider in regard to lease arrangements: length of lease, amount of monthly rent, right to sublease, and lessee responsibility for utilities and other expenses. A long-term with an option to renew would add considerably to the value of the shop.

Example

Step 1: Review and make a comparative analysis of income and expense for the previous three years.

Income and Expense Summary
for 12 months ending June 30

	19x6	19x7	19x8
Net Sales	$ 43,422	$ 67,455	$ 69,998
Cost of Sales	19,540	30,355	31,499
Gross Profit	23,882	37,100	38,499
Operating Expenses	18,105	29,680	30,199
Net Operating Profit*	$ 5,777	$ 7,420	$ 8,300

* Depreciation, excessive owner compensation, and interest added back.

Note: It is important to consider income and expense trends as well as the current year's (19x8) data. To more accurately predict future economic trends, the valuator should review the most recent five years of financial data.

Step 2: Adjust the balance sheet to reflect the market value of tangible assets.

Balance Sheet Summary
as of June 30

	19x6	19x7	19x8	Restated at Market Value on Value Date
Assets				
Current Assets:				
Cash	$ 9,758	$ 10,488	$ 15,521	$ 15,521
Inventory	58,332	79,996	93,009	93,009
Total Current Assets	68,090	90,484	108,530	108,530
Fixed Assets:				
Trade Fixtures,				
Leasehold Improvements,				
and Equipment (net)	23,440	18,211	24,100	35,850
Total Assets	91,530	108,695	132,630	144,380
Liabilities	41,969	44,650	47,230	47,230
Net Tangible Equity	$ 49,561	$ 64,045	$ 85,400	$ 97,150

Example 261

Step 3: Apply the formula.

Formula Valuation Using Net Operating Profit Multiplier

Net Operating Profit (Fiscal year end 6/30/x8)	$ 8,300
Annual Multiplier	× 1.5
Indicated Value of Intangible Assets	12,450
Plus Adjusted Market Value of Assets	
Current	108,530
Fixed	35,850
Total Gross Value	156,830
Less Liabilities	47,230
Net Equity Value	$109,600

Sources of Further Information

Associations

American Video Association
557 East Juanita #3
Mesa, AZ 85204
(602) 892–8553

Video Software
Dealers' Association
3 Eves Drive, Suite 307
Marlton, NJ 08053
(609) 596–8500

Publications

Articles

Martin, D. R., "Room for One More?," *Video Store Magazine,* June 1986, pp. 72, 74, 78, 80.

Outcalt, Richard F.,"Putting a Price Tag on Your Business," *Video Store Magazine*, May 1985, pp. 58, 62, 64.

Shaw, David A., "Buyer's Market," *Video Store Magazine,* October 1986, pp. 42–46.

Books and Pamphlets

Almanac of Business and Industrial Financial Ratios, Prentice-Hall, Englewwod Cliffs, N.J., 1986.

*Annual Statement Studie*s, Robert Morris Associates, Philadelphia, 1986.

Trade Journals

American Video Monthly
22222 Sherman Way, Suite 100
Canoga, CA 91303
(818) 702–9707

Dealerscope Merchandising
North American
Publishing Company
400 #1 Totten Pond Road
Waltham, MA 02154
(617) 890–5124

Home Video Publisher
701 West Chester Avenue
White Plains, NY 10604
(914) 328–9157

Music/Video Retailer
210 Boyston Street
Chestnut Hill, MA 02167
(617) 964–5100

Retailer News/Video Software Dealer
249 E. Emerson Avenue, Suite G
Orange, CA 92665
(714) 921–0600

The VCR Letter
Paul Kagan & Associates
126 Clock Tower Place
Carmel, CA 93923-8734
(408) 624–1536

Video Business Magazine
345 Park Avenue South
New York, NY 10010
(212) 686–7744

Video Marketing Newsletter
1680 Vine Street, Suite 820
Hollywood, CA 90028
(213) 462–6350

Video Software
Dealers Magazine
5519 Centinela Avenue
Los Angeles, CA 92665
(213) 306–2907

Video Store Magazine
Harcourt, Brace, Jovanavich
1700 E. Dyer Road, Suite 250
Santa Ana, CA 44130
(714) 250–8060

About the Authors

Glenn M. Desmond and *John A. Marcello* are professional business appraisers. Mr. Desmond is a member of the American Institute of Real Estate Appraisers where he holds the MAI professional designation, and a member of the American Society of Appraisers, with the ASA designation. Mr. Marcello is also a member of the ASA, where he holds the senior ASA designation.

Both authors are involved on a daily basis in the valuation of closely held businesses. Their clients include some of the largest corporations in the United States, as well as owners of medium-sized and small businesses; attorneys and other professionals representing business owners; and many governmental agencies, including the U.S. Deparment of Justice, the Internal Revenue Service, the General Services Administration, and state and local public agencies. They have qualified as expert witnesses in hundreds of valuation proceedings in both federal and state courts.

Mr. Desmond is the author of the internationally marketed *Business Valuation Handbook*. In addition he has authored a textbook entitled *How to Value Professional Practices* and a number of monographs on specialized subjects. Mr. Desmond frequently lectures throughout the United States on business valuation subjects. He is the developer of and instructor for the Business Valuation Seminar series sponsored by the American Institute of Real Estate Appraisers.

The authors maintain an active national business valuation practice. In valuing smaller businesses through the years, the authors faced the continual frustration, common to all business appraisers, of attempting to obtain meaningful market data on actual sales of small, privately held businesses to compare with the business being appraised. The *Handbook of Small Business Valuation Formulas* reflect's the authors' many years of accumulated experience in solving this dilemma and summarizes their observations with respect to valuation formulas and rules of thumb.